WHAT YOU WILL FIND IN THIS BOOK

Casino Gambling addresses three long-standing controversies head-on:

- Does card counting really work in today's blackjack shoe game?
- Can a controlled throw really alter the random outcome of casino craps?
- Do dealer signatures really exist in casino roulette?

Casino Gambling teaches recreational gamblers easy-to-use methods for increasing their chances of winning at blackjack, craps, roulette, baccarat, and the other popular table games.

Recreational and serious gamblers will find methods herein for:

(1) Gaining an advantage at blackjack by exploiting biases engendered by the non-random shuffle;

(2) Gaining an advantage at craps by executing a controlled throw of the dice; and

(3) Gaining an advantage at roulette by determining and playing into a dealer signature.

The book provides all gamblers with the author's valuable secrets for successful mental preparation and play: developing a winning attitude, self-confidence and the discipline it takes to maximize your chances of walking with a win or holding your losses to a minimum.

The book presents the facts for gambling on the Internet—current status, problems confronting gamblers, and future direction.

And much, much more!

Casino GAMBLING

A Winner's Guide
to Blackjack, Craps,
Roulette, Baccarat,
and Casino Poker

JERRY L. PATTERSON
with Eric Nielsen and "Sharpshooter"

A Perigee Book

A Perigee Book
Published by The Berkley Publishing Group
A division of Penguin Putnam Inc.
375 Hudson Street
New York, New York 10014

Copyright © 2000 by Jerry L. Patterson
Book design by Tiffany Kukec
Cover design by Miguel Santana
Cover photograph copyright © by I. Burgum/P. Boorman/Tony Stone Images

First edition: February 2000

Published simultaneously in Canada.

The Penguin Putnam Inc. World Wide Web site address is
http://www.penguinputnam.com

Library of Congress Cataloging-in-Publication Data

Patterson, Jerry L.
    Casino gambling : a winner's guide to blackjack, craps, roulette, baccarat, and casino
poker / Jerry L. Patterson 1st ed.
        p.   cm.
    "A Perigee book"—T.p. verso.
    ISBN 0-399-52511-4
    1. Gambling. 2. Casinos. I. Title.

GV1301.P29   2000
795—dc21
                                                                99-055268
                                                                CIP

Printed in the United States of America

10   9   8   7   6   5   4   3

The reader should be advised that games of chance and sports betting are illegal in certain jurisdictions. The publisher and the authors urge the reader to determine the legality of any such game in his or her state before engaging in any gambling activity. The methods and procedures outlined in this book have been developed by the authors based on their own research. However, games of chance always present the possibility of risk and financial loss, and all recommendations and procedures are made without any guarantees by the authors or publisher. The authors and publisher disclaim all liability incurred in connection with the use of this information.

To the memory of five departed friends:

Steven Heller, who taught me that winning starts in the mind, not with a method;

George Stanton, a fabulous raconteur in the classroom and over a glass of beer afterward;

Howard Kaplan, Damon Runyon's legacy who couldn't quite make it over the hump but gave it a hell of a shot trying;

Richard Hoffman, a great guy to hang out with and to have at my table in the heyday of shuffle tracking;

John Painter, nobody knew more about sports betting systems and methods—nobody. Jack's memory and lessons live through his hundreds of recorded audio tapes.

And to Harvey Oliver.

CONTENTS

X ■ CONTENTS

SECTION SIX
CASINO POKER, OTHER CASINO GAMES, AND GAMBLING ON THE INTERNET

CHAPTER NINETEEN
Casino Variations of Traditional Poker

CHAPTER TWENTY
Casino Variations of Blackjack

CHAPTER TWENTY-ONE
Gambling on the Internet

Acknowledgments

This book would not have been possible without the help of two associates—both successful advantage players, both trained in the scientific method, both qualified gaming researchers, both major contributors to this book:

Eric Nielsen, a successful professional blackjack player in the early 1990s, turned his attention to roulette and took a new approach by defining the dealer as the basis of his research. Three years of hard work produced a solution—advantage methods he named Signature Series Roulette. Eric proved conclusively that the dealer is, in fact, the factor, and the dealer signature proved to be the basis for his solution to the game. Eric is gratefully acknowledged for sharing one of these advantage methods with the readers of this book—the Power Sector Method. Eric also contributed to the roulette state-of-the-art chapter and to Chapter 2 on attitude, self-control, and discipline.

"Sharpshooter" (who wishes to remain anonymous), a degreed mechanical engineer and president and founder of an engineering consulting company in the Midwest, was researching the mechanics of controlled throws of the dice a couple of years before I became seriously involved in the mid-1990s. Sharpshooter is acknowledged for his development work on controlled throws, which is the foundation of the advantage method described in this book. His brilliant calculations reveal the precise advantage that the skilled rhythm roller can achieve.

I would also like to acknowledge Bob Bowser. When Bob looks at a blackjack game, his intense analytical mind and powers of observation allow him to see the game as few others do. This is why I asked him to write Chapter 4 on why the non-random shuffle leads to exploitable biases in the shoe game. Those readers looking for a rationale of why biases lead to winning tables and why they should consider changing their traditional card counting approach, should study this chapter carefully.

Many have speculated as to who is the most dangerous casino player in the industry. I suggest that a new breed of players known as advantage players are most deserving of this notoriety.

Advantage players will utilize any approach, strategy, ploy or method to derive a legitimate advantage.

—STEVE FORTE

Introduction

Before getting to the reasons for this new edition, let's sum up what we mean by the term *advantage* as it pertains to casino gamblers.

An *advantage player* is the gambler most feared by the casino because they know he or she can beat them and beat them consistently. Casinos are virtually powerless to thwart the advantage player (unless they bar him or her from the casino). An advantage player actually holds an advantage over the casino. An advantage is a statistical edge—a percentage edge over a specific casino game.

The bottom line is winning, and I will show you in this book not only how to develop an advantage in blackjack, craps, and roulette, but also how to exploit that advantage with betting tactics and money management. You will also learn to recognize other advantage players, and exploit them to your own advantage.

WHY THIS BOOK WAS REVISED

In 1982, when the first edition of this book was published, my primary game was blackjack. Sure, I was interested in the other table games offered at that time—craps, roulette, and baccarat—and played them as a diversion. But, I, like the gambling public, always believed that you could not beat the house, that the casinos hold an insurmountable advantage in craps, roulette, and baccarat. How wrong I was about craps and roulette.

In the intervening years, I and my two associates who assisted me in writing this edition — Eric Nielsen and Chris Pawlicki — have thoroughly and exhaustively researched advantage methods for craps, roulette, and baccarat.

The first reason that this new edition was written is to share this information with both recreational and serious gamblers — to teach them that it is possible to gain an advantage over the house in craps and roulette as well as blackjack. We use the term advantage player to define the gambler who has achieved this status.

Before I get to the second reason this new edition was written, let me explain what I mean by advantage for craps and roulette.

Craps

At the craps table, the stickman pushes the dice over to the player. The player picks up the two cubes and tosses them toward the far end of the table. They hit the front wall, bounce off, and come to rest with one of 36 possible combinations showing on top. Most gamblers, myself included, believed that this outcome was always random. You will learn in this book that this random outcome can be altered, that the dice can be controlled in such a way to achieve an advantage for the player.

Roulette

The roulette wheel is spinning; the croupier picks up the ball and launches it into orbit around the wheel. The ball slowly loses velocity, drops from its orbit, and falls into one of 38 pockets at the bottom of the wheel. Is this event random? Or is the result predictable? You will learn in this book that the dealer may get into a "muscle memory groove" to make his or her spins predictable. We call this a *dealer signature*, and finding one can lead to a player advantage.

Scientists claim that if a phenomenon is not random, it is predictable. In craps, we alter the random outcome by controlling the dice. In roulette, we search for and exploit dealers whose games are yielding non-random results. Both games therefore become predictable and, in this book, we will disclose those factors that lead to accurate predictions, to an advantage, and to winning.

Baccarat

Baccarat, however, is different. Many gambling authors who write about baccarat would have you believe that an advantage can be obtained by exploiting the streaky nature of the game, by betting on a streak of player or bank wins or on its termination. However, we could not find a solution to the game after reviewing scores of alternatives.

Blackjack

Blackjack is different, too. Scores of books have been written that claim card counting delivers an advantage in the multi-deck shoe game. The card counting process involves a system that tracks the status of the remaining decks to be played; when the remaining cards favor the player (are heavy in 10s, face cards, and aces), the card counter increases the bet size to capitalize on the player advantage on the next hand. Conversely, when the remaining cards favor the dealer (are rich in low cards, which reduce the chances of the dealer breaking), the card counter bets small in anticipation of the dealer's advantage and therefore the counter's higher probability of losing that hand.

You will learn in this book that although the player may have a theoretical long-term advantage, it disappears in actual casino play for all but a handful of very experienced and skilled counters because of the card clumping introduced by the non-random shuffle.

The second reason for writing this book, therefore, is to dispel the myth that card counting works in the multi-deck blackjack game and to describe an advantage method that exploits the non-randomness inherent in the shuffle, which leads to a bias that is advantageous to the player.

The third reason for updating *Casino Gambling* is to give an overview of the new table games, including the many variations of casino poker games. Many new table games have been introduced by the casinos since the first edition of this book was published back in 1982. The most popular are Spanish 21, Caribbean Stud, Pai Gow Poker, Let It Ride, and Three Card Poker; all of these games will be covered in this book.

A SUMMARY OF WHAT YOU WILL LEARN IN THIS BOOK

Chapter 1 is "A Walk Through the Casino." Many changes have transpired since I wrote this chapter for the original edition and called it "a guided tour through the casino." The biggest change you'll notice on the casino floor is the abundance of slot machines—a much higher percentage of floor space has been allocated to them because they're much more profitable than the table games. On this walk-through, we'll be avoiding the slot areas, observing all the table games, and commenting on advantage players as well as the games themselves.

Chapter 2 is the first step of your winning program. I can teach you how to achieve an advantage in this book, but it's no good without discipline and self-control. We'll start by defining the problem called "casino mind ploys" and then describe two approaches for achieving the level of discipline necessary to become a consistent winner.

Casino blackjack is covered in Chapters 3 through 8. Beginning players should start with Chapter 3, which explains how the game is played as well as presenting an interesting historical background. Chapter 4 gets to the nub of the problem and addresses the blackjack controversy head-on: card counting versus the non-random shuffle in the multi-deck shoe game. The state of the art in single- and double-deck card counting systems are also addressed. An alternative to card counting is introduced and justified in Chapters 5 and 6 and then described in Chapter 7. In Chapter 5, you will learn why the non-random shuffle engenders card clumping and exploitable biases. In Chapter 6, I extend this analysis and prove why player-favorable games exist. Finally, in Chapter 7, the winning method for the multi-deck shoe game is presented. Card counting works very well in the single- and double-deck games. Alternative methods for achieving an advantage over the casino, one of which utilizes existing card counting techniques, are described in Chapter 8.

Casino craps is covered in Chapters 9 through 14. Recreational players unfamiliar with the game should start with Chapter 9, "Basic Craps." The concept of a controlled throw, or *rhythm roll* as it's also called, is introduced in Chapter 10. Before you learn how to achieve an advantage via a controlled throw, you will see the calculation and learn how to measure your advantage in Chapter 11. Thus armed, you learn the two-step process of executing the controlled throw in Chapter 12. Chapter 13 describes three betting tactics for operating in the advantage zone, while Chapter 14 concludes the craps section by disclosing additional ideas for maintaining and enhancing your advantage.

Casino roulette is covered in Chapters 15 through 17. Beginning players should read Chapter 15 first. Chapter 16 describes the state of the art in roulette advantage systems, including the authors' research and development activities in the dealer signature arena. The winning method, called the Power Sector Method, is described in detail in Chapter 17.

Baccarat basics and some ideas for system play are presented in Chapter 18. Despite extensive research, my associates and I uncovered no advantage methods for casino baccarat. With only two betting decisions—player or bank—and mechanical house rules for taking an additional card on player and bank hands, no factors emerged from our research that might predict which way the next hand would go. However, since baccarat is a "streaky" game, we do offer some ideas for system play for the recreational gambler interested in playing the game.

Because of their similarity, the popular poker variation games—

Caribbean Stud, Let It Ride, Three Card Poker, and Pai Gow Poker—are all included in Chapter 19. The chapter begins with a brief history of standard poker, which concludes with the reasons why the casinos introduced the poker variation games. Standard poker, which is a whole field unto itself, is outside the scope of this book. Readers interested in learning how to play and win at standard poker should consult the *Gambler's Book Club Catalog* for a wide range of book choices. But since the ranking of standard poker hands is the basis for the poker variation games, it is delineated prior to the description of each of the poker variation games.

Chapter 20 describes other new games introduced by the casinos in the last two decades of the twentieth century, games that are variations of traditional blackjack. They are Single-Deck Blackjack Dealt to the Bottom, Double Exposure Blackjack, Multiple-Action Blackjack, and Spanish 21. There is no known way to achieve an advantage in these games, but the recreational gambler will find them simple and fun to play, and the serious gambler may find them a pleasant diversion from traditional blackjack.

Chapter 21 takes a look at the present and future of gambling on the Internet. Casinos are operating on the Internet as this book goes to press, but their future is uncertain. The pitfalls of gambling on the Internet, both its casinos and sports books, are presented for the interested reader.

The appendix summarizes the casino gambling courses and services offered by the author and his associates.

HOW TO READ THIS BOOK

Both occasional and frequent gamblers will find a wealth of winning material in this book. I suggest you read it through once from cover to cover. Serious students of gambling methods should then go back and study one of three games in detail in which an advantage over the casino can be achieved—blackjack, craps, or roulette.

If your game is multi-deck blackjack, after learning and reviewing the basics of the game in Chapter 3, study Chapters 4 through 7, paying particular attention to the advantage method description in Chapter 7. If you're in a position to play in casinos that offer single- and double-deck blackjack, study Chapter 8 as well. Be sure to review Chapter 2 before your first casino trip after studying these chapters.

If your game is craps or if you want to learn craps from A to Z, study Chapters 10 through 14 after learning the basics of the game in Chapter 9. Pay particular attention to the advantage method description in Chapter 12 on the rhythm roll. Have a pair of dice at hand as you study Chapter 12 so you can learn the basics of setting and throwing the dice. Be sure to review Chapter 2 before your first casino trip with the new data.

Readers interested in achieving an advantage at roulette should focus on Chapters 16 and 17 after learning the basics of game from Chapter 15. In this chapter you'll also find Oscar's Grind, a very useful, simple-to-use method.

If you're a recreational player, I believe you will find it fun and interesting to select at least one advantage method in this book and make an attempt to learn it. Especially recommended is the controlled throw described in Chapter 12.

Read on and reap!

Section One

BECOMING AN ADVANTAGE PLAYER

One

A WALK THROUGH THE CASINO

Before we begin our quest to become an advantage player, let's take a walk through a typical large casino, one that might be in any major casino area such as Las Vegas or Atlantic City, and observe what's going on. We'll use this opportunity to make some opening comments about the games themselves—and who knows, we might just run into one or two advantage players.

As we walk in, we are confronted by a sea of slot machines and an incessant cacophony: the whir of spinning wheels, the clanking of coins falling into trays, bells sounding when jackpots and other winning hands are hit, and the shrieks and yells of lucky winners. Ignore all this and let it become a rhythmic blur in the background. We didn't come here to play the slots with their high casino advantage (in some cases as high as 17 percent).

Let's find our way through this maze of machines and walk onto the main casino floor. Pausing to get our bearings, we see crowds of people and a sea of tables, most with players sitting, but a few long, oblong tables surrounded by standing players. Where to begin? Noticing the hanging signs identifying the game being played, we walk over to the roulette area first.

ROULETTE

The first things we notice are the large electronic displays that show the last 21 numbers that have hit. The other things we notice are the players. They seem to be betting haphazardly; some are putting chips on the outside of the layout ("outside bets"), betting that a red or black number will hit, an odd or even number, or a high or low number. There are 38 numbers on the wheel, including the two green zeros, and these outside bets pay even money (you win the same amount as you bet). If you think about it, you can see the house edge right away for these bets: As long as any one of your 18 numbers hits, you win, but, with the two green zeros winning for the house, there are 20 chances out of 38 for you not to win. There's the house edge: 2 additional chances out of 38 for the casino to take your money, which equates to an advantage of about 5¼ percent (you can think of this as about 5 percent of all the money bet going to the casino). For those casinos that only take half of your outside bet when one of the green zeros hits, the house edge drops to about 2¾ percent.

The players betting on specific numbers or combinations of numbers on the inside of the layout seem to be dropping their chips at random, some making as many as a dozen bets in hopes that they'll get lucky on the next spin. We'll describe what these bets are and how they're made in a later chapter, but for now, let's look at one player in particular.

Unlike the others, he scans the electronic displays for just 15 or 20 seconds, then moves quickly to one of the spinning wheels with the ball already in motion and places a green chip, straight up, on each of five numbers. The croupier calls, "No more bets please," and the man waits patiently for the ball to land. It falls on one of his numbers and he exudes quiet satisfaction with his win. The dealer pushes 35 green chips over to him. "That one's yours," he says to the dealer, pointing to the green chip on the winning number. The other players glance at him with admiration. Paying no attention to them, he picks up his chips and quietly walks away, melting into the crowd. At the cashier's cage he cashes in for a total of $875—a quick profit of $750 after subtracting the $125 he bet.

Was this a lucky hit or what? No. This player, with a keen understanding of the number positions on the wheel, had detected a "power sector" on the electronic display—certain numbers hitting with regularity in one sector of the wheel. His experience told him that this was a strong dealer signature and he knew he had an advantage in this game.

This man is an advantage player.

CRAPS

Walking away from the roulette wheels, we hear cries of excitement: "Winner! Winner! Winner! Take the don'ts, pay the line, eight came easy. Coming out, same good shooter. Craps, eleven, horn bets, whirl bets, highs and lows, place your bets. Let's go, throw an eleven, shooter."

What's all the shouting about? Amidst all the excitement, we see a cluster of players crowded around a large oblong table—a craps table, the most exciting of casino games. You can get more action and more bets down at the craps table in five minutes than you can at roulette or blackjack in an hour.

Belly up to the table and watch the shooter roll the dice. Notice the pass-line bet on the layout, one of the best bets, because the casino advantage is only about 1.4 percent. If you're a beginning player, you're probably somewhat confused by all the shouting and the myriad of bets confronting you on the layout. But, for now, place a $5 bet on the pass line and go with the shooter. After the come-out roll, it's a very simple matter to understand—a 7 or 11 wins on that first roll, called the "come out," while a 2, 3, or 12 loses. All other numbers are points—4, 5, 6, 8, 9, 10—and the shooter's objective is to repeat that point number, 6 for example, before a 7 is rolled. If he or she rolls a 6, you're paid even money—$5. If a 7 is rolled, the dealers quickly scoop up the losing bets, including yours.

We'll get to a more detailed description of the game in a later chapter, but for now notice a tall lanky man step up to the table, to the spot where it's his turn to throw the dice next. On his roll, he gets the dice and holds them for 45 minutes. This means that he is not throwing the losing 7. He rolls number after number and is winning on almost every roll. The other players shout and scream for this shooter to roll the point. Racks are filling up with chips.

What's going on here? Is this shooter just lucky? No. Take a closer look at this shooter. He doesn't just pick up the dice and throw haphazardly down the table like most of the other players do. Using one hand as prescribed by the casino, he carefully positions the two die as they lie on the table in front of him, so that certain combinations of numbers show on the top and bottom and on each of the other two sides. Then he picks them up and releases them with a nice easy rhythm so they gently tap the back wall.

His objective? To avoid the losing 7. He's a rhythm roller with an advantage over the casino.

After his 45-minute roll, the man places his stacks of black, green, and purple on the table and requests a "color up." The boxman counts down the chips and places seven orange ($1,000 chips), two black ($100 chips), and three green ($25 chips) on the table. After acknowledging the accolades from the other players and then nonchalantly tossing three $25 chips to the dealers, the man picks up the chips and walks to the cashier's cage.

This man is an advantage player.

CASINO POKER

Before you get too excited, let's take a walk over to the other gaming and see what's going on.

Forgetting to look for the sign identifying the blackjack pits, we notice some other gaming tables that are not immediately recognizable. Let's take a closer look at these games, new to the casinos in the last decade of the twentieth century, and see what's going on here.

At the first table, a dealer is dealing seven cards to each player; the players each pick them up and arrange them into two poker hands: a normal poker hand of five cards and a hand of two cards. This is Pai Gow Poker, which differs from normal poker in that the players play against the dealer, not among themselves. With one exception we'll discuss in a later chapter, the hands have the same value as normal poker. We'll get to a full description of these hands later, but for now the main difference between Pai Gow Poker and normal poker is how you set your hand. You arrange your seven cards into a five-card hand and a two-card hand. To win, both your five-card hand and your two-card hand must beat the dealer's five-card hand and two-card hand.

As long as we find ourselves in the poker area of the main casino floor, let's take a look at some other new poker games. After talking to a friendly casino *floor person* (who watches the games to ensure that payoffs are made correctly and no cheating occurs), we learn there are three other variations of poker called Caribbean Stud, Let It Ride, and Three Card Poker. All of these games are played on blackjack-like tables, all played against the house. Specific rules vary among the games, but we learn that the main feature of each game is player bonuses for various types of poker hands. For example, a winning hand of three-of-a-kind pays 3 to 1 at Caribbean Stud and Let It Ride, and 4 to 1 at Three Card Poker.

BLACKJACK

Now on to the tables where most of the players seem to be concentrated. Blackjack is the most popular casino table game. Most tables feature the multi-deck shoe game with all player cards dealt face up. The game is simple enough to play: You win if your hand has a higher value than the dealer's hand or if the dealer breaks (goes over 21) and you don't. The value of your hand is determined by adding up the face value of all your cards (face cards count 10 and aces count 1 or 11). Starting with your initial two cards, you can decide to hit (take another card), stand, double your bet and take only one more card, or split a like pair and play two hands with a like bet on the second hand.

We'll get to more details on playing the game in a later chapter, but for now, let's observe another player as he slowly walks up and down the aisles checking each blackjack table in turn.

At some tables, this player pauses to observe a hand or two, but then moves on, unsatisfied with what he sees. After examining every table on the casino floor, he starts over in his table examination.

This man is a card counter, a *back counter* in blackjack jargon. He's waiting for the count to reach a certain level before entering the game. He counts low cards as $+1$ and high cards as -1 and keeps a running count from hand to hand and round to round at each table where he observes one or more rounds of play. If the count reaches a plus number equal to or greater than the number of decks remaining to be dealt from the shoe, he enters the game believing he has an even game or an advantage because there are a few more high cards than low cards left in the shoe. Otherwise he doesn't play.

Let's follow this player as he finds an acceptable game. It's eight decks, two have been played, and the count is $+10$ as he takes a seat. The $+10$ means that there are 10 more high cards than low cards remaining to be played. And since high cards are more valuable to the player than the dealer, theoretically at least, this player has an advantage, albeit a very small one.

Our man notices the two other players in the game as he makes his first bet of $25.

He wins the first bet, plays a few more hands, losing most of them as the count skyrockets with bunches of low cards being dealt in the next few rounds, leaving the extra high cards in the shoe and yielding a theoretical advantage on the next hand.

He works his bet up to $300 on each of the two hands he is playing. He's dealt a 20 on one hand and a pair of 4s on the second. He splits the 4s and pulls a 5 to the first, making a total of 9. Where are those extra high cards, he thinks? He doubles down on the 9 and pulls a 10 for 19. On the other 4, he pulls more small cards, ending with a stiff hand of 16. But he's not worried because the dealer shows a 6 and will undoubtedly turn over a hole card of 10 and then break because of all the extra 10s in the shoe.

The dealer turns over a 3 for a total of 9, and then she deals herself a 2 to the hand, which now totals 11. By this time the man's heart is pounding as he "sees" that 10 coming out of the shoe to make the dealer hand a 21. But it doesn't happen. The clumped low cards keep popping up. She pulls a 5 for a total of 16. "Now the 10," he feels like yelling out. But unfortunately it's not to be as the dealer pulls a 5 for a 21, wiping out his total bet of $1,200 on the two hands.

Is this man an advantage player? Is his card counting method an advantage system in the eight-deck game? You'll learn in this book that the player was playing into a clump of low cards caused by the non-random shuffle. Low cards are advantageous to the dealer because she hits her hand last, after all the players have made their decisions, and has much less chance of breaking. We'll discuss this further in Chapter 4.

BACCARAT

On the main casino floor, we need to look at one more game—baccarat. Let's step into the subdued elegance of the baccarat pit. Notice the deeper-pile carpets, the richly upholstered armchairs, and tuxedo-clad dealers. The game and environment are quiet and calm in the European tradition.

The game is easy enough to play and can be learned in a few minutes by examining any of the casino gaming guides. Only two simple decisions are required: How much to bet and whether to bet on the player or the bank to win the hand.

Baccarat is designed to appeal to a different class of player—the high roller. We may see many players with huge stacks of chips in front of them, perhaps with $20,000, $30,000, and more. These special-breed players are here to risk serious money. They didn't need to be coaxed into putting it on the line. Their egos demand it. So, accordingly, the casino provides a very dignified atmosphere for these big players. That's why the dealers dress in tuxedos and there are no noisy slot machines nearby. Gourmet buffet tables are sometimes provided right in the room. The surroundings are lavish. Attentive waiters, waitresses, and pit personnel service the players with first-class treatment.

If you decide to play baccarat, I suggest trying it at the mini-bac tables located on the main casino floor. You won't get the same treatment as the high rollers, but the minimums are much lower. Many casinos offer $5 minimum games.

POKER

Stepping off the main casino floor, we find the poker room. Poker rooms are purposefully set apart from the main casino floor. In poker, the casino simply provides a dealer, a table, and a legal venue for players to take each other's money. For this service, the casino takes either a percentage of each pot or charges rent (rake), depending on the type of game being played. The casino's money is never at risk (a really sweet deal for the casino, when you think about it). With poker, the casino has no need to psych out the players, so it provides a quiet, dignified environment and caters to their each and every whim—anything to keep them playing, because the longer a player plays, the more commission or rake the casino makes. In some poker rooms, massage therapists offer their services to players, who sometimes sit in marathon games for 24 hours or more. That's right—back rubs while you play!

This finishes our walk through the casino. But before getting to the main order of business, you need to learn how to prepare mentally before sitting down to play.

Two

MENTAL PREPARATION FOR BECOMING AN ADVANTAGE PLAYER

Trying to consistently beat casinos at the games they offer has historically been a losing bet for the general public. Just look around at the grand, lavishly built, multimillion-dollar casinos in which you play. They're built with and profit from the millions of dollars players lose each day.

This should be pretty obvious, but sometimes even the savviest players take this important fact too much for granted. And very few understand the real factors that make this whole thing a harsh reality.

Do you want to know what's really going on here? What the casinos are doing to rake in big profits? How they subtly manipulate players to empty their pockets? And, more important, do you want to learn how to recognize and counter these clandestine little ploys? If so, then follow along for an eye-opening lesson in casino mind ploys.

CASINO MIND PLOYS

Most players know that each casino game is designed with a theoretical mathematical edge that favors the house. Most people believe this is how casinos make their money. For example, a slot machine may be preprogrammed to pay out 90 percent—yielding a 10 percent gross profit for the house. Or, in roulette, the house maintains an edge of around 5 percent on every bet or combination of bets, which yields around $5 for the house on every $100 wagered.

Most casual players just accept this and play with the hope they'll get lucky and hit a jackpot or perhaps go on a rare extended win streak. They come to the casino prepared to risk their bankroll for the elusive big score. If they fail, they usually rationalize the loss by writing it off as the cost of entertainment.

What most players don't know is that the built-in house edge is not how casinos take in the majority of their money. Most of their take comes from the invisible "mind ploys" they routinely use on players. The casino's ultimate goals are to get players to (1) stay longer than they should; (2) bet more than they can afford to risk; (3) give back what money they do manage to win; and (4) generally play with poor control, little confidence, a lack of discipline, and no money management.

As mentioned previously, the built-in house edge for roulette is around 5 percent. Yet the casino's typical roulette take is well in excess of 20 percent! In blackjack (playing with basic strategy) the house edge is advertised at only around 1 percent or 2 percent. Yet the take here is also in excess of 20 percent.

How do they do it?

By devising all sorts of hidden gimmicks to get players to spend it all—the compounding effect of betting the bankroll over and over again. These ploys are very powerful, very discreet, and very effective. They should be learned and highly respected. No player, no matter how experienced, is immune.

As a simple example of a commonly used ploy, have you ever played a table game and had the floor person pleasantly offer you a free meal just as you're preparing to depart the game? Did you notice that it took 15 minutes or more for your comp voucher to come? The floor person probably came back smiling a few times to say, "Your comp will be ready in just another minute or so." Well, in many cases, this is an orchestrated casino ploy designed to squeeze a little more action out of you—probably more than you're prepared to risk. Most players naturally feel obligated to continue playing while waiting for their comp. So the ploy works, and we see it used routinely throughout the casino industry. Who knows how many millions of dollars this one little trick strips from players' pockets?

The casinos use dozens and dozens of similar tricks. Virtually all novice and recreational players are totally unaware of them. Even the majority of serious players are not able to spot these aspects of casino play.

A few more examples: Ever notice that the only places to sit down in a casino are right at the gaming tables or in front of a slot machine? Ever notice that the background noise levels in the poker room are different than in the main casino? Ever notice that the air quality in a casino has a rejuvenating effect? Ever notice that you can hear lots of people talking and laughing, even at 5:00 A.M. when the casino is nearly empty? Ever notice how easy it is to justly overspend your bankroll in a casino? Ever notice how the casino environment makes you feel like a kid in a candy store? Ever notice how easy it is to tap your savings account or credit line in a casino? Ever notice how the mortgage or rent money doesn't seem so important in a casino environment? Ever notice how you feel as if you can play for hours on end in a casino? Ever notice how you believe your extended losing streak simply cannot continue, so you increase the size of your wagers, hoping to make it all back quickly? These thoughts, feelings, and perceptions are the result of carefully orchestrated casino mind ploys brilliantly created and executed to influence your behavior.

To win consistently for an extended period of time, a player must become an advantage player. And to become an advantage player, one must become skilled with special playing methods to overcome a game's mathematical edge. That's the subject of this book. But playing methodology is only one portion of the overall winning formula. An advantage method is not quite enough by itself. With a winning method alone, most serious players still tend to lose in the long run. Again, casino mind ploys serve as the main culprit.

This subject is worth exploring further, so we solicited the help of Dale Patterson (no relation to the author), a psychologist and authority on human behavior, especially the behavioral effects of casino-type influences such as lighting, sound patterns, imagery, and suggestion.

Together, we spent significant time in Atlantic City observing and studying the ploys used in today's ultramodern casinos. As you might imagine, Dale had a field day with this project. He was successful in identifying an entire new generation of mind ploys—most of them technology based. Things such as air quality, noise levels, sound patterns, colors, graphics, and even aromas were identified as having dramatic influences on player behavior.

Dale was intrigued and amused with the carnival-like atmosphere on the main casino floor. Typically, the casino floor is crowded with recreational gamblers who normally have a fixed amount of cash to spend. It's the casino's job to get them to risk it all—and when it's gone, to make a trip or two to the ATM or American Express machine for more cash. They successfully accomplish their goal by creating a diversionary, carnival-like environment. Dale explains it this way:

> The deliberate carnival-like atmosphere takes most people back, subconsciously, to a time when they were youngsters, a time when responsible behavior was not a concern. As youngsters at a carnival, we couldn't normally get into too much trouble. We have parents to supervise us and control our behavior, especially spending. Think about what would likely occur without that supervision and spending limitation. We would go wild, buying all the cotton candy and hot dogs we could eat. We would go on every thrill ride over and over again. We would see every side show.

Now, envision this carefree mentality in the body of an adult with cash in his or her pockets and with credit cards at hand, in a casino loaded with exciting games of chance, and huge prizes as a potential reward. Most people will subconsciously submit to this childish frame of mind—it's usually just a matter of how much time it takes. In this state of mind, normal people will toss responsibility out the window and spend like crazy with no consideration for the consequences. They'll lose all discipline, take wild risks, and chase losing bets until it's all gone. The more time they spend in the environment, the deeper they get hooked. When they finally leave the casino (after some number of hours), gamblers will settle back into a more normal state of mind and, if the casino session was a loser, will feel remorse. But it's too late. The casino has the money.

In addition to the overpowering carnival-like atmosphere, Dale noted other subtle ploys. The carpet designs in most casinos are wild. This irritates the eyes, forcing patrons to look up and get involved with the exciting action. Some new slot machines are adorned with colored, bubbling water towers to lure players and keep them depositing coins. Dale also noticed a distinct change in the air quality throughout different parts of a casino, suggesting that perhaps an oxygen-enriched environment is used in gambling areas. All of these factors contribute to a feel-good, carefree environment.

All of this brought to mind a story I had recently heard concerning a player who was in a downtown Las Vegas casino at 4:00 A.M. Although he only saw one or two people standing around, he heard the sounds of lots of people talking and laughing. It turns out the casino was piping in recorded background sounds over a speaker system to create the illusion of a lot of people having a good time—enhancing the carnival atmosphere.

It's important for you to recognize these and any other ploys so you can counteract them mentally. The key to gaining the upper hand is to properly prepare beforehand, to have a plan of action and make some decisions that put you in control, not the casino.

DEVELOPING A GAMBLING PLAN OF ACTION

Time and money management are the keys to becoming an advantage player, for staying there, and for any short-term approach to a casino gambling session.

I like to express these ideas as eight decisions that a player must make prior to each gambling session. Making these decisions will establish the discipline that most recreational gamblers lack, but that most winning gamblers possess:

- Decision 1: To play or not to play

- Decision 2: Which casino to play

- Decision 3: Which game to play

- Decision 4: Which table to play

- Decision 5: What basic betting unit size to use and tactics for increasing the bet

- Decision 6: When to leave the table

- Decision 7: When to leave the casino

- Decision 8: When to terminate the casino session

Taken together, these eight decisions constitute a gambling plan of action for your gambling session. You should think about each one before leaving home and write down the parameters of each decision. I recommend you use a small, three-ring notebook. But even if you don't write down your decisions, at the very least think them through. Let's examine each decision in detail.

Decision 1: To Play or Not to Play

You must be in the proper physical and mental frame of mind before you play. Are you tired? Emotionally upset? If you are, you should seriously consider not playing at this time because your risk of losing is high. The casinos will always be there—go when your energy level is normal or high and you are mentally ready to exercise the discipline to win. Tired or emotionally upset gamblers risk losing their discipline to stick with a plan of action. If this happens, you are usually beaten before you start.

Decision 2: Which Game to Play

Most gamblers have a favorite game they play the majority of the time. Blackjack is the most popular, followed by craps, roulette, and baccarat. But reading this book probably indicates that you are interested in learning to play and win at one or more games. Choose the game you feel you have the best chance of winning at, or the game you are going to practice. If you decide to play more than one game, allocate the time you plan to spend on each. For example, you may plan to spend an hour or so playing blackjack and then hit the craps tables to practice your controlled throw for a while. This all sounds mundane, but it's important to think it through before your session to establish discipline.

Decision 3: Which Casino to Play

If you have a choice of casinos, choose one with a greater number of tables and less crowded conditions. For blackjack, the more tables you can scout, the more chance you'll have to find a player-favorable game. The same goes for roulette—more tables equals a greater chance of finding a dealer signature or power sector. If you're playing craps, you want to find uncrowded tables so you can get more turns with the dice to practice your controlled throw.

If you live close to a casino location and play often, you should assess the conditions at your local casinos; find out which times are best to play within your own playing constraints.

Decision 4: Which Table to Play

Are you going to use blackjack's winning factors to scout for and find player-favorable games? Are you going to scout for a power sector? Practice your controlled throw? This decision ties into which table to play, but keeping it as a separate decision in your winning plan of action is a key part of your approach to the discipline I'm stressing in this chapter.

Decision 5: What Basic Betting Unit Size to Use and Tactics for Increasing the Bet

Making this decision starts with a basic money management policy—the size of your bankroll and the number of units into which you break it. I recommend a 100-unit bankroll (with $100, one unit would therefore equal $1), but I realize that aggressive gamblers will go for 50-unit bankrolls and some even less. I know gamblers who leave home with $200 and bet with $5 and $10 units (a 40-unit or 20-unit roll). The fewer the units, the higher the risk of tapping out, so it's best to accumulate a 100-unit or at least a 50-unit bankroll before you take off for the casinos.

If you've been gambling awhile and read other books, you've read this policy elsewhere, but it's important enough to repeat here: Establish a gambling bankroll with money you can afford to lose and then set it aside for strict use at the tables.

Risk Level. Once you've defined your unit size, think about the level of risk that you wish to take when raising your bet. Are you aggressive? Do you want to go for the jugular when you get into a hot game? Or will you play it conservative, settling for less of a win, but not giving back a whole lot when you do get ahead or not losing as much when things don't break your way?

Betting Strategy. Now decide on which betting strategy you are going to employ. I recommend choosing one of the strategies I suggest in the following chapters, but if you're a recreational gambler and have a betting strategy that has worked well for you over the years, by all means use it.

Decision 6: When to Leave the Table

How do you know when it's time to leave a table? There are three criteria to use:

Depart on a Game Breakdown. In blackjack, if you find yourself playing into a strong dealer bias and losing most of your hands, it's time to leave. Don't wait for things to turn. Strong dealer biases can last for hours. Get away quickly.

In craps, if you're having trouble in executing your controlled throw and suffering too many quick seven outs, it's time to leave. If you're playing for fun, remember Huey Mahl's words of wisdom: "We are exposed to the vagaries of dice for very short periods in the overall scheme of things." Anything can happen in the short term. The table may be in a losing trend and this losing trend could continue even though, in the long run, things will even out to the small house edge. If you don't believe that craps tables exhibit trends, observe several games in your next session. You'll see hot tables, cold tables, and choppy tables.

In roulette, if the power sectors are not sustaining and you are not hitting early on, call it off and move on to another game or take a break.

Depart on a Stop-Loss. Part of this decision process is establishing a stop-loss, a point previously established where you decide to quit gambling after losing a certain amount of money. How many betting units will you lose before you quit playing and depart? I've discussed stop-loss considerations with each betting tactic described in this book. You need to review them and adopt the ones that fit the level of risk you are prepared to take.

Depart on a Stop-Win. This is a concept foreign to many gamblers, but very important nonetheless. A stop-win is the opposite of a stop-loss. A stop-win can occur in one of two ways: (1) You have set a win goal for this session and accomplished that goal; (2) you're in a hot game and have experienced a nice win.

Decision 7: When to Leave the Casino

If you have a choice of casinos, leave when the tables are crowded or when you have difficulty finding a winning table in blackjack, a craps table where you can get the dice quickly, or a roulette table where power sectors are hitting. Go to a casino with better conditions.

If you're locked in to a one-casino location, be careful. If playing conditions are bad, keep your bet sizes small and respect your stop-loss point. Keep in mind that every unit you save, every unit you don't lose, looks that much better, especially after a losing session because you've cut your losses short. Never give back a win when you're confronted by poor playing conditions. This is the time to go to the video poker machines and have some fun playing with quarters.

Decision 8: When to Terminate the Casino Session

There are three good reasons to terminate a gambling session:

- You have reached the limit of your optimal session time. You need a break to keep your perspective and your control. In many years of working with my gambling students, I have found that optimal session time is around 90 minutes. Give it a try.

- When you are just plain tired and this is affecting your judgment and play.

- When you've incurred serious loss. For example, if you've lost your discipline and dropped a session bankroll at one table, don't dig for more money. Leave and take a break. Assess the situation.

We call these eight decisions a winning paradigm. Taken together, they constitute a plan of action for your casino trip or session. To conclude this chapter, I'll expand this winning paradigm to include 16 axioms of successful gambling. Follow these in conjunction with the advantage methods in this book and join a very small but elite group—advantage players!

SIXTEEN AXIOMS OF SUCCESSFUL CASINO GAMBLING

1. **Bankroll.** Establish a formal bankroll that is separate from your other personal financial accounts. It is not to be relied on to pay personal bills or any nongambling-related expenses. If the worst happens and the bankroll goes, then life will proceed normally in other areas. This is one of the most important (and most frequently violated) rules of successful play.

2. **Practice.** Before risking money in a casino, become familiar with your game or games by first reading and practicing at home. Become proficient and confident with your chosen play strategies prior to live-action play.

3. **Take frequent breaks.** Remember, the longer you expose yourself to the casino environment, the more susceptible you become to their mind ploys. You're only human and can withstand just so much. Generally, individual playing sessions should be limited to ninety minutes, no more than two hours, and daily playing limits should be established at four hours. A nice long break between playing sessions (outside the casino) is essential.

4. **Play only at peak efficiency.** This means rested, feeling well, feeling confident, and in a positive state of mind. Avoid playing when you feel ill, negative, dull, or tired.

5. **Don't play under the influence of alcohol.** If you do, have a friend or spouse with you, give him or her your wallet, and play to a strict stop-loss. It's too easy to reach for the roll of bills or a credit card after a cocktail or two. It is also advised not to play immediately after a large meal.

6. **Get comfortable.** Spend an adequate amount of time getting used to the casino environment before jumping into a game. It is advisable to avoid playing during the first hour after arriving by car. If you've flown in for a trip of several days, try not to play for at least three or four hours after arriving.

7. **Avoid playing near the end of a trip or session.** On a trip of several days, avoid playing during the last four hours. Players tend to rush in situations like this and, as a result, lose discipline and money. On a day trip, avoid playing during the last hour.

8. **Don't use credit.** You should avoid using casino credit (or any other credit source) to fund your bankroll. If you can't help it, then at least handle your credit line with discipline and always respect your stop-loss point.

9. **Stay current.** Keep up on new gaming developments and state-of-the-art systems. Things evolve quickly in this business.

10. **Avoid the comp game.** Be careful when offered freebies and favors from casinos, unless your main reason for gambling is to enjoy the "high life." Complimentary rooms and meals are nice perks, and you should graciously accept them when they are offered. But don't get wrapped up in the comp game if you're a serious advantage player. Many players give the casinos action just for the comps. This is a losing proposition. Unless you are a recreational player or high roller who enjoys the attention, your only objective should be to win money.

11. **Leave your ego at home.** Many players lose significant sums of money making foolish bets to impress other players, casino personnel, or themselves. They stay in bad games too long, bet over their heads, or do something equally dumb. It's a part of our basic human nature (our ego) that drives this sort of behavior. We're all subject to it. But as astute players, we must learn to control it. In the morning, no one else but you

is going to remember that you were playing black chips, when your bankroll only supports green.

12. **Avoid superstitious behavior.** It's very easy to get wrapped up in unhealthy superstitions and weird compulsive behavior in a casino. Having a lucky charm at the table is okay, but wringing your hands, tapping the table three times, tugging your left ear, rolling your head, and crossing your legs before each new round of cards borders on problem behavior. Learn to rely on your skill and mental acuity, not superstitions, to win.

13. **Document your play.** After each table, jot down a few notes about the game, the casino, the time of day, the casino conditions, the table conditions, the play strategy you employed, your win or loss, and anything else you feel may be pertinent. When you return home, organize these play records. After several sessions, you will begin to see patterns in your performance. Analyze your records and make adjustments in your play to eliminate the losing trends and enhance the winning trends. Soon, you'll be playing with optimal personal efficiency. You will also be in a solid position to establish realistic future expectations for your own personal play.

Good documentation (and the ongoing analysis of that documentation) is essential for consistent winning and very helpful in maintaining a high degree of confidence in the casino.

14. **Be human.** It's okay to make a mistake or two, here or there. It's okay to lose discipline every so often. It's okay to take a wild gamble every once in a while. We're only human. Play smart and strive for perfection, but settle for excellence. Don't be too hard on yourself.

15. **Develop a long-term business plan.** Just as serious businesspeople do, consider your gambling activities as a formal business with the objective of turning a handsome profit. Establish a formal plan, similar to your individual trip plans, but extended into the future. Plan your trips, project your profits, estimate your expenses, and open a dedicated bank

account. Do it up right. This will clarify your long-term objectives and keep things in organized perspective.

16. **Give something back.** Once you've developed some playing skill, consider taking someone under your wing. There's no better way to master a skill than to teach it.

Section Two

BLACKJACK

Three

BLACKJACK BASICS

HISTORY

Gambling with playing cards spread steadily throughout Europe after Johann Gutenberg printed the first deck of cards in Germany in 1440, and many of the games involved drawing cards to reach a certain total. Although the exact relationship remains obscure, blackjack is believed to have evolved from several of these early games. Baccarat, with the magic number of 9, appeared in Italy about 1490, followed by the game of "seven and a half," which seems to be the first game where the player automatically lost if he went over the desired number.

The game of "one and thirty" was first played sometime before 1570 in Spain, and the Duke of Wellington, the Marquis of Queensbury, and Prime Minister Disraeli all played *quince* (15) in Crockford's, the famous English casino that flourished between 1827 and 1844. From France came *trente et quarante* (30 and 40) and finally *vingt un* or *vingt et un* (21 or 20 and 1), which crossed the Atlantic Ocean and was listed in the *American Hoyle* of 1875.

As first played in the United States, blackjack was a private game, but by the early 1900s, tables for 21 were being offered in the gambling parlors of Evansville, Indiana. Acceptance was slow, and to stimulate interest, operators offered to pay 3 to 2 for any count of

21 in the first two cards, and 10 to 1 if the 21 consisted of the ace of spades and either the jack of spades or the jack of clubs. This hand was called, of course, blackjack. The 10-to-1 payoff was soon eliminated, but the term remained, first as the name of any two-card 21 hand, and subsequently as the name of the game itself, although 21 would have been more appropriate.

By 1919, tables covered with green baize and emblazoned in gold letters announcing "Blackjack Pays Odds of 3 to 2" were being manufactured in Chicago and appeared in illegal gambling halls throughout the country. The popularity of the game grew slowly until gambling was legalized in Nevada in 1931, and blackjack soon became the third-most-successful game, outstripping faro, but trailing both roulette and craps. Because of the prohibitive casino edge of 5.26 percent in roulette, discouraged players drifted away from the game, and by 1948, blackjack had become the second-biggest casino moneymaker after craps.

TODAY'S GAME

In 1956, Baldwin, Cantey, Maisel, and McDermott published a book called *Playing Blackjack to Win* (Barrows, 1956) which contained a nearly perfect basic strategy. This was followed by Edward Thorp's book *Beat the Dealer* (Vintage Books, 1966), which refined the strategy and added a counting system. Now, for the first time, the sophisticated gambler could learn to play nearly even with the house, and perhaps with a slight edge in his or her favor. This scientifically developed information sparked a nationwide interest in blackjack that made it the number one table game in America beginning in the 1960s and continuing through the '70s, '80s, '90s and into the new millennium.

Because the table is less than half the size of those required for craps, roulette, or baccarat, with a corresponding reduction in both the number of players and casino personnel, blackjack is far less intimidating to the beginning player. Couple this with the simplicity of the basic rules—both the player and the dealer draw cards and whoever comes closest to 21 without going over wins—and you can understand the popularity of the game. Actually, as of this writing, the popularity is actually diminishing a bit. Casinos are introducing variations to traditional poker and blackjack that compete with blackjack tables for space and players.

Blackjack is unique among the casino games inasmuch as any player can make decisions that will affect the results of the game. In addition, it is the only game where the outcome of one hand influences the following hands. Since the type of cards that have been played determines the value of the cards remaining to be played, the probability of winning or losing is in a constant state of flux, and although chance is still a significant factor, the skillful player enjoys a marked advantage over the novice. Obviously, the casinos are a profit-making institution, so why do they continue to offer a game where the player has a fair chance? Elementary, my dear reader, because over 90 percent of all players do not make a sufficient effort to learn the fundamentals of the game. Ironically, the fact that the game can be beaten is well known to the casino operators, but since very few players will be bothered to invest the necessary time to learn to play, blackjack and its variations have become the most profitable table games in the house.

An Overview

New casinos are still being designed and built in Nevada, Atlantic City, and other casino locations across the country, and hundreds of new casino gamers are trying their luck every day. Many of these neophytes know little or nothing about how to play or how to bet. To accommodate these newcomers, as well as the multitude of existing players who are not playing to their best advantage, let's thoroughly explore the basic elements of the game.

First of all, although you will find seven betting spots on the table, blackjack is not a group game. Each bettor is playing against the dealer and betting against the house; the number of players or where they sit has no effect on the ultimate outcome. Second, the decision to draw or not draw by any one player has no long-run effect on other players. Of course, in any one hand, the player to the right of you or the dealer appears to have significant control of the results of your hand, but really, the draw of each player at the table has an equal effect on the hand. Nevertheless, many players critically observe the play of the hand preceding the dealer, commonly called "third base," with the result that most beginners shun this chair to avoid contention.

Ninety percent of the bettors are there to enjoy themselves, and because of the game's frequent pauses for shuffling, dealing, and settling bets, you'll find an air of relaxation not always found at the other games. So if you happen to sit where there are disagreeable players, move to another table. They are almost always plentiful.

As soon as you sit down, you'll need chips. Place some currency alongside the betting circle directly in front of you. The dealer will announce the amount to the pit supervisor and exchange it for distinctly decorated clay disks, setting them in front of you as he pushes your money through the slot in the table into the concealed drop box. All the tables carry $1, $5, and $25 chips frequently colored white, red, and green, and some tables keep $100 chips, usually black. The dealer's rack also contains half dollars, but these are used only for settling odd bets such as the 3-to-2 payoff for a blackjack on a $3 or $5 wager. If you want to change a large-denomination chip for smaller ones, place it alongside your betting spot and announce, "Change, please." Never place it in the circle, as it may be mistaken for a bet.

Although state regulations in New Jersey and most other gambling locations prohibit betting with cash, money wagers may be made in some casinos in Nevada, even though most prefer the use of chips. Skillful dealers can add up the value of a stack of mixed chips in an instant because of the various colors; however, all currency is green and the bills must be checked and rechecked. Casinos also realize that many bettors subconsciously do not place the same value on chips that they do on actual cash. Somehow many people feel that once they give up their money for chips, it's not really theirs anymore; subsequently players find it infinitely easier to push out four green chips than to reach in their wallet and extract a $100 bill.

Most gaming locations have regulations that prohibit using chips from one casino in another. This practice used to be prevalent in Nevada, but was discontinued because of *junketeers*. These players were required to buy in for a certain sum in order to qualify for complimentary rooms, meals, and travel. However, they frequently reneged on their obligation to play at the house tables, and would go play at other casinos with the same chips. Now, every casino has its own chips, so you'll have to convert to cash before you leave the casino.

As you stack your chips, you may notice one or two small signs displayed near the dealer. One often lists the casino's particular blackjack rules, and the other indicates the minimum and maximum bets in effect at that particular table. Minimum bet sizes may be $2, $3, $5, $10, $15, $25, $50, and $100, but $2 and $3 minimums are often hard to find; the most common table size seems to be $5 or $10. Although maximum bets usually range up to $1,000, pit bosses have special signs available for high rollers, and $2,000 or $3,000 maximums are not unusual. Occasionally, the entire table will be roped off for a really big bettor.

All bets must be placed before any cards are dealt, and many casinos will permit additional wagers in adjacent vacant positions. Procedures for betting more than one hand vary from casino to casino, so check with the dealer if this type of betting appeals to you. Incidentally, when you have finished playing, the dealer can't reconvert your chips into money, but he will be more than willing to change them for larger denominations. The term for that request is "Color me up." For cash, you must take your chips to the cashier's cage.

BASIC GAME PLAY

Blackjack can be played with one to eight decks of cards. Before a new game begins, the dealer spreads the new cards to be used

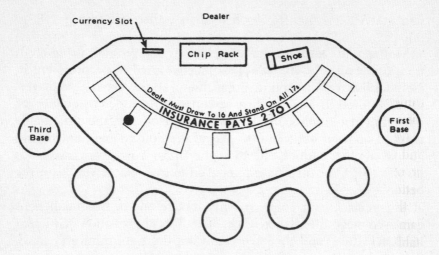

FIGURE 1: *Blackjack Table Layout*

across the table, first face down so the backs can be inspected for telltale markings, and then face up, enabling both the dealer and the players to ascertain that there are no extra or missing cards. Refer to Figure 1 for the standard blackjack table layout. Standard 52-card poker-sized decks are used, and the four suits have no significance; only the numerical value of each card is important: 2s through 9s are counted at their point value, and all 10s and face cards are valued at 10. The ace is unique, and can be counted as 1 or 11 at the player's option.

Then the dealer thoroughly shuffles the one to eight decks of cards. Upon finishing, the player is given a colored cut card, to be inserted anywhere in the stack of cards, which is placed on the table but held by the dealer. Some people prefer not to cut, and the option is then given to the next player. If no one wants to cut, the dealer does it himself. After the cut is completed, the dealer places the colored card toward the back of the stack to indicate when to reshuffle. If it's a single-deck game, the dealer holds the cards and deals; if it's a multi-deck game, the cards are placed in a wooden or plastic dealing box called a *shoe*. In any case, the first card—called a *burn card*—is not used, but is placed on the bottom of the single deck or in a discard rack. The burn card is not usually shown, but in many cases the dealer will expose it if a player asks to see it.

The dealer starts with the player on his left (often called *first base*) and continues in a clockwise direction. He deals each player and himself one card; then he deals each player a second card. However, his second card is dealt face down, under his up-card. Both of the players' cards are usually dealt face down in the single-deck game and face up in multi-deck play, but whether the cards are exposed or not, the game is played in the same manner. Although many bettors prefer the single deck with its feeling of secrecy as they peek at their cards, the trend is overwhelmingly toward the multi-deck game. Not only is faceup play much faster, and therefore more profitable for the casino, but since bettors are not permitted to touch their cards, the opportunity for player cheating is nearly eliminated.

When everyone has his or her initial two cards, again starting at first base, each bettor is permitted to draw additional cards, which are always dealt one at a time, face up. If the player goes over 21, he loses; his bet is collected, and his cards are placed with the rest of the discards. After each player has acted on his or her hand, the dealer must then complete his own hand based on fixed rules printed on the table covering. These usually include hitting (taking a card) on all 16s, and standing on all 17s (the exception is that in most handheld games, the dealer hits the soft 17—A, 6). The players' exposed hands do not affect the dealer's play; his decisions are mechanical. If the dealer does not go over 21 (going over 21 is called *breaking*), he collects from players with hands totaling less than his; pays off players with hands better than his; and ties, or *pushes*, with players holding hands of equal value.

Now you are ready for the next hand, which is dealt from the remaining cards. This continues until the colored cut card appears, signaling a reshuffle after the completion of the hand in progress, and the entire procedure is repeated.

As you play, you may notice a well-dressed person with an air of authority casually observing the dealer, the players, and the action;

this is the pit boss or floor person, who is responsible for a group of tables and settles all disputes. His decisions are final.

Basic Blackjack Terms and Procedures

Standard blackjack terms are defined here to describe how to play the game.

Blackjack. After receiving your initial two cards from the dealer, you determine their value by simply adding them together. A 5 and 3 is 8; a king and 6 is 16; and an ace and 7 is either 8 or 18. If your first two cards consist of an ace and a 10 or any picture card, the hand is a perfect one—a "blackjack"—often called a *natural.* Unless the dealer ties you with another blackjack, you have an automatic winner, and instead of the usual even-money payoff, you are immediately paid one and a half times your bet. For example, if you have $10 up, you receive $15. With a tie, called a *push,* no money is exchanged.

Hard and Soft Hands. All hands not containing an ace are known as *hard* hands, and any hand including an ace that can be valued as 11 is called a *soft* hand. For example, an A, 5 is a soft 16; if hit with a 2, the hand becomes a soft 18. If another card is drawn (for instance, a 9), the ace is revalued as 1 (if it were valued as 11 you would break) and the final hand now becomes a hard 17. Any hard hand of 12 through 16 is known as a *stiff* or *breaking* hand, because it is possible to go over 21 with the addition of just one more card.

Standing. The player always has the option of *standing* (refusing additional cards) at any time. The usual procedure is to give a hand signal rather than a verbal one. To indicate to the dealer that you wish to stand, simply wave your hand palm down over your cards. Just remember that in Atlantic City and many other places where multi-decks are used, you are never permitted to touch your cards or your initial bet. The dealer will then move on to the next player. In many Nevada games the cards are dealt face down and the players pick them up to play the hand. A standing signal in this game is given by tucking your first two cards dealt (the ones you are holding in your hand) under your chips.

Hitting. If you are not satisfied with the total of your hand, you may draw one or more cards, as long as you don't break, or go over 21. To call for a hit, either point at your cards or make a beckoning motion with your fingers. In the Nevada facedown game, scrape your two cards toward you on the felt to call for a hit. When the hit card breaks your hand, the dealer will automatically scoop up your bet and place your cards in the discard tray, as you have lost, even if the dealer subsequently breaks. If you break in the Nevada facedown game, just toss your two held cards to the dealer—face up.

Splitting Pairs. When the first two cards you receive are of equal value, you may elect to split them and play each as a separate hand, drawing until you are satisfied or break. You play the card on your right first and then the card on your left. Two 10-value cards such as a king and jack can also be split, but when aces are split, most casinos permit drawing only one card to each split ace. If a 10-value card is drawn to a split ace, or vice versa, the resulting hand is considered as 21, not a blackjack, and is paid off at 1 to 1. This 21 would tie any dealer 21 but would lose to a dealer blackjack. In many casinos, if a pair is split and a third card of the same rank is drawn, the hand may be resplit. To indicate to the dealer your desire to split, merely slide up another bet of equal value next to your first wager, touching neither your cards nor the original bet. In the Nevada facedown game, just turn over your pair and put out the extra bet.

Doubling Down. When you think that with just one more card in addition to your first two you will beat the dealer, you are allowed to double your original bet and draw one, and only one, more card. While many casinos will permit you to double down on any initial hand except two cards totaling 21, some restrict this option to hands that total 10 or 11. To signal the dealer your intention to double down, place another bet up to the amount of the original wager alongside your first bet. In the Nevada facedown game, turn your two cards over and put out your extra bet. Since you will always

have the advantage when you take this option, you should double for the full amount. Again, to minimize the chances for player cheating, you are not permitted to touch either your cards or your original bet (except to turn the cards face up). When you split a pair, many casinos will permit you to double down after you draw the first card to each of the split hands.

Insurance. Whenever the dealer's up-card is an ace, before proceeding with the hand, she will ask, "Insurance, anyone?" If you believe the dealer's hole card is a 10 for a blackjack, you are permitted to place a side bet up to half of your original wager on the Insurance line in front of you. If, indeed, the dealer does have a 10 in the hole, you are immediately paid 2 to 1 on your insurance bet, but lose your original wager unless you too have blackjack and tie the dealer. You are not really insuring anything; you are simply betting that the dealer's unseen card is a 10. The only time I recommend taking insurance is when you have a blackjack and are past the third level of a winning progression (a succession of winning hands). I'll discuss winning progressions in a later chapter.

Surrender. A few casinos offer the option of surrender. If you are not satisfied with your chances of beating the dealer after seeing your first two cards, you may announce "Surrender" and the dealer will pick up your cards and collect half your bet, returning the other half to you. This is the only decision in blackjack that is indicated verbally.

When the dealer is required to first check his hole card for blackjack, the option is called "late surrender." If you are permitted to turn in your hand before the dealer checks for blackjack, the deci-

sion is termed "early surrender." In some casinos, you must announce your surrender decision before the dealer deals to the first
hand.

Dealer's Play. After offering cards to all players, the dealer ex-
poses her hole card. If there are players who still have not broken,
the dealer then acts on her hand according to fixed rules, with none
of the player options. When the dealer's cards total 17 or more, she
must stand, and with a hand of 16 or less, the dealer must hit until
she reaches 17 or better. If the dealer breaks, all remaining players
win. In most casinos, the dealer must count an ace in her hand as
11 if it will raise her hand to 17, 18, 19, 20, or 21. A few casinos
make an exception to this rule and require the dealer to hit A, 6,
or soft 17. It is important to note that the dealer has no choice in
the matter. If all the players have hands totaling 18, 19, 20, or 21,
the dealer must still stand with a 17 — an obvious loser. Likewise,
if the players show hands totaling 12, 13, 14, or 15, the dealer must
still hit her 16 and risk breaking an otherwise winning hand. If the
dealer does not break and reaches a hand between 17 and 21, she
collects the bets of the lower hands, pays even money to the higher
hands, and pushes or ties the equal hands (which she indicates by
tapping the back of her fingers in front of the player's cards). Players
are now free to pick up their winnings, if any, and make a new bet
as the whole process is repeated.

BASIC STRATEGY

Before we get into a basic strategy for blackjack, let's consider the
objective first. Many blackjack books define the objective as getting
a hand as close as possible to 21. This is not always true. Your
objective is to beat the dealer, and learning this lesson is your first
step on the road to becoming a winning blackjack player. It is possible to beat the dealer by holding a hand that totals less than 21 — a
12 or 13, for example. Remember, there are two ways to win: by
holding a higher hand than the dealer, and by not hitting a breaking
hand and waiting for the dealer to break. This is a decision that

many beginning players seldom make. Thinking they must always get as close as possible to 21, they hit more often than they should, thus breaking, losing more often and contributing to the casino edge of up to 6 percent over the non–system player.

Casino rules are defined to give the dealer one major advantage and one major disadvantage. His advantage is that he always draws last. If he breaks after you have broken—in reality a tie—he has already collected your chips, and he does not return them. The dealer's disadvantage is that he must draw if he has 16 or less; therefore, with hands totaling 12 to 16, it's possible that the next card may break him. You, the player, can capitalize on this handicap by making judicious decisions about drawing or standing.

While many players lose because they hit too often, other novices, unrealistically hoping for the dealer to break, do not hit enough. These hitting and standing decisions cannot be made by hunch; logic must be used. If the dealer's up-card is 2, 3, 4, or 5, you know she must hit, no matter what the value of her *hole* (facedown) card is; therefore, you should stand on a lower hand value, such as 13, and hope for the dealer to break. On the other hand, if the dealer has a high up-card (for instance a 9 or 10), you would hit and try to get as close to 21 as possible. This is because there is a good chance that the dealer's hole card is also high, and with a hand greater than 16, the dealer must stand.

Most occasional gamblers are unaware of the tremendous amount of research that has been done to provide blackjack players with optimal strategies for playing the hands. This research has been performed with the aid of high-speed computers by some of the best mathematical minds in the country.

The resulting strategy, designed to win more of your good hands and lose fewer of your bad hands, takes the casino advantage over you down to an absolute minimum if you follow the decisions for standing, hitting, splitting, doubling down, and surrendering. To understand the strategy, though, you must remember the three variables involved in making blackjack decisions—your two cards and the dealer's up-card. There are 550 possible combinations of these three variables, but many of these decisions are similar, and about 30 rules cover all of them.

The small differences among the basic strategies result from the use of more decks in the game and the rules variations among the casino locations. In general, the multi-deck strategy is more conservative than the single-deck strategy. An example is the player hand of 11 versus a dealer up-card of ace. In the single-deck game, with just 52 cards, the player has a better chance of drawing the 10, so the correct play is to double down. More cards in the multi-deck shoe game reduce the chances of drawing the 10, so the correct play for this game is to hit instead of doubling down.

Many blackjack books advise never to deviate from basic strategy. Their reasoning is that you should always make the correct mathematical play for every hand. This reasoning is correct if you play for the long run. In this book, however, I am teaching you to play for the short run. There are occasions when you should deviate from basic strategy either to protect your locked-up, short-run profits or to avoid the risk of doubling down or splitting on hands that only slightly favor the player.

In the meantime, until you get further along with your blackjack study, I recommend that you learn the basic strategy thoroughly so that you can play the hands automatically, without even thinking about them. Basic strategy deviations occur infrequently, and if you are uncertain about how to play any hand, basic strategy is always the correct play. If you would like a wallet-sized card to carry with you on your casino visits, I will be happy to send you one for no charge. Just use the form in the back of this book to request it.

Basic Strategy for Standard Multi-Deck Shoe Blackjack

Typical casino rules for the standard multi-deck shoe games are as follows:

- Double down on any two cards
- Split pairs up to four times

- Double down permitted after splitting

- Dealer stands on soft 17 (A, 6)

- Insurance permitted

- Surrender not permitted

The basic strategy for the standard multi-deck shoe game is shown in Exhibit 1.

Exceptions to the standard game usually involve doubling after splitting and surrender. If the casino does not permit doubling after splitting, make the following modifications to basic strategy:

- 2, 2: Split on dealer up-cards 3–7, not 2–7

- 3, 3: Split on dealer up-cards 4–7, not 2–7

- 4, 4: Hit on dealer up-cards 5–6, do not split

- 6, 6: Split on dealer up-cards 3–6, not 2–6

If the casino permits surrender, surrender on the following hands:

- 9, 7 and 10, 6 against a dealer ace

- 9, 6; 9, 7; 10, 5; 10, 6 against a dealer 10 or face card;

- 9, 7 and 10, 6 against a dealer 9

The standard multi-deck strategy can also be used in the two-deck game with the following exceptions:

- 9: Double down on dealer up-card of 2–6; not 3–6;

- 5, 6 or 7, 4: Double down against a dealer ace; hit if your 11 is 9, 2 or 8, 3

Basic Strategy for the Multi-Deck Shoe Game
(Doubling Down After Splitting Permitted)

THE DEALER'S UP-CARD

YOUR HAND	2	3	4	5	6	7	8	9	10	A
8	H	H	H	H	H	H	H	H	H	H
9	H	D	D	D	D	H	H	H	H	H
10	D	D	D	D	D	D	D	D	H	H
11	D	D	D	D	D	D	D	D	D	H
12	H	H	S	S	S	H	H	H	H	H
13	S	S	S	S	S	H	H	H	H	H
14	S	S	S	S	S	H	H	H	H	H
15	S	S	S	S	S	H	H	H	H	H
16	S	S	S	S	S	H	H	H	H	H
17	S	S	S	S	S	S	S	S	S	S
A,2	H	H	H	D	D	H	H	H	H	H
A,3	H	H	H	D	D	H	H	H	H	H
A,4	H	H	D	D	D	H	H	H	H	H
A,5	H	H	D	D	D	H	H	H	H	H
A,6	H	D	D	D	D	H	H	H	H	H
A,7	S	D	D	D	D	S	S	H	H	H
A,8	S	S	S	S	S	S	S	S	S	S
A,9	S	S	S	S	S	S	S	S	S	S
A,A	P	P	P	P	P	P	P	P	P	P
2,2	P	P	P	P	P	P	H	H	H	H
3,3	P	P	P	P	P	P	H	H	H	H
4,4	H	H	H	P	P	H	H	H	H	H
6,6	P	P	P	P	P	H	H	H	H	H
7,7	P	P	P	P	P	P	H	H	H	H
8,8	P	P	P	P	P	P	P	P	P	P
9,9	P	P	P	P	P	S	P	P	S	S
10,10	S	S	S	S	S	S	S	S	S	S

H = Hit. S = Stand. D = Double Down. P = Split.

EXHIBIT 1: *Basic Strategy for the Standard Multi-Deck Shoe Game*

Basic Strategy for Standard Single-Deck Blackjack

Typical casino rules for the standard single-deck game are as follows:

- Double down on any two cards
- Split pairs up to four times
- Double down not permitted after splitting
- Dealer hits soft 17 (A, 6)
- Insurance permitted
- Surrender not permitted

The basic strategy for the standard single-deck game is shown in Exhibit 2.

A Practice Drill for Basic Strategy

Using a single deck of cards, place one card face up in front of you; this is the dealer's up-card. Now flip over two cards at a time. Each of these two-card pairs is your hand. Make a basic strategy decision for each hand against this same up-card. Deal through the entire deck. Now shuffle the deck, change the up-card and repeat the drill. Choose up-cards that may be giving you problems in remembering. Do not play out the dealer's hand in this drill.

An alternative procedure for this drill is to deal three cards at a time: an up-card and your two-card hand. Play against a different up-card for each two-card hand dealt.

This drill can be varied to work on various aspects of basic strategy. For example, to practice pair splits, set up a special training deck loaded with extra 2s, 3s, 4s, 5s, 6s, and 7s. To practice doubling on 9, 10, and 11, load up a training deck with extra 4s, 5s, and 6s.

To practice playing stiff hands, load up a training deck with extra

Basic Strategy for the Las Vegas Game
(Single Deck)

THE DEALER'S UP-CARD

YOUR HAND	2	3	4	5	6	7	8	9	10	A
8	H	H	H	D	D	H	H	H	H	H
9	D	D	D	D	D	H	H	H	H	H
10	D	D	D	D	D	D	D	D	H	H
11	D	D	D	D	D	D	D	D	D	D
12	H	H	S	S	S	H	H	H	H	H
13	S	S	S	S	S	H	H	H	H	H
14	S	S	S	S	S	H	H	H	H	H
15	S	S	S	S	S	H	H	H	H	H
16	S	S	S	S	S	H	H	H	H	H
17	S	S	S	S	S	S	S	S	S	S
A,2	H	H	D	D	D	H	H	H	H	H
A,3	H	H	D	D	D	H	H	H	H	H
A,4	H	H	D	D	D	H	H	H	H	H
A,5	H	H	D	D	D	H	H	H	H	H
A,6	D	D	D	D	D	H	H	H	H	H
A,7	S	D	D	D	D	S	S	H	H	S
A,8	S	S	S	S	D	S	S	S	S	S
A,9	S	S	S	S	S	S	S	S	S	S
A,A	P	P	P	P	P	P	P	P	P	P
2,2	H	P	P	P	P	P	H	H	H	H
3,3	H	H	P	P	P	P	H	H	H	H
4,4	H	H	H	D	D	H	H	H	H	H
6,6	P	P	P	P	P	H	H	H	H	H
7,7	P	P	P	P	P	P	H	H	S	H
8,8	P	P	P	P	P	P	P	P	P	P
9,9	P	P	P	P	P	S	P	P	S	S
10,10	S	S	S	S	S	S	S	S	S	S

H = Hit. S = Stand. D = Double Down. P = Split.

EXHIBIT 2: *Basic Strategy for the Standard Single-Deck Game*

10-value cards and remove all neutral cards (7s, 8s, and 9s). This drill is limited only by your imagination.

This is only a partial training program. For a complete program that includes drills, exercises, and memory aids, refer to my book *Blackjack: A Winner's Handbook*. Information on how to obtain this book is located in the appendix.

Table Selection, Table Departure, and Betting Strategies for the Recreational Player

The advantage methods described in Chapters 7 and 8 can be easily learned by most recreational blackjack players. The knowledge gleaned just by reading these chapters, even if not practiced and executed exactly, will keep you away from many losing games. Here are three key ideas to keep in mind:

Table Selection. When selecting a table to play, don't just enter the first game you come to with an open seat. Observe the table for evidence of winning. These are the three key words — *evidence of winning*. Do the players have chips in front of them? Are they happy? Are they talking to one another? If not, look for another game. This idea is expanded upon in Chapter 7, where blackjack's winning factors are discussed in detail.

Table Departure. Many recreational players do not depart a table until they have lost their buy-in amount. This is not smart play. It's exactly what the casinos want you to do, just as I have discussed under "Casino Mind Ploys" in Chapter 2. We have learned, over the years, that if a player goes in the hole for three betting units, there is very little chance that he will leave the table a winner. What this simply means is that if you're a $10 bettor and buy in for $100, you should leave the table if you find yourself down $30 at any point during the game. The key words here are *three-bet stop-loss*. If you're down three bets, why stay to lose? Why give them your full buy-in amount of $100? Depart and find another game. This idea is expanded upon in Chapter 7.

A Basic Betting Strategy. Have you ever noticed how other players raise their bets? Some increase after a losing hand. Others increase after a winning hand. With others, it's a guessing game as though they're trying to divine what the dealer will do in the next hand. My advice is to *flat-bet* (bet the same amount) until you're three bets ahead of the dealer. If you're a $10 bettor, wait until you've won $30 before considering raising your bet. So *three* is also the key word for this idea. Win three bets before you increase. How much should you increase? For now, consider just 25 percent. For example, if you're betting $10, increase to $13 and try to win three more bets, then increase another 25 percent (from $13 to $17). Don't worry about betting in two colors of chips. Just ask the dealer to change some $5 chips into $1 chips. We'll discuss this more in Chapter 7.

Now, let's jump into the advantage arena. Our discussion of advantage blackjack begins in Chapter 4 with a discussion of the state of the art of advantage systems. To further your understanding of the advantage method discussed in Chapter 7, I explain how and why the non-random shuffle can engender exploitable player biases in Chapter 5. And, since the advantage method described in Chapter 7 involves searching for and playing in player-favorable and dealer-breaking games, I define these biased games and offer proof that they exist in Chapter 6. The recreational player or occasional gambler who may not be interested in this background information may prefer to skip right to Chapter 7.

Four

STATE-of-the-ART ADVANTAGE BLACKJACK SYSTEMS

The current state of the art in blackjack advantage systems is confusing and overwhelming to the new player. Scores of card counting systems confront the beginning player. Controversies and contradictions abound among card counting authors and those authors who have gone in a different direction (this one among them for the multi-deck games). The controversies boil down to the following two questions:

- Does card counting work in the multi-deck shoe game?

- Does the non-random shuffle create exploitable player biases in the multi-deck shoe game?

To get the answer to the first question, it is necessary to understand what happened when the Atlantic City casinos opened in 1978.

CARD COUNTING IN THE MULTI-DECK SHOE GAME

The opening of the Atlantic City casinos and the very favorable rules that they featured has been well documented in my book *Blackjack: A Winner's Handbook.*

The *early-surrender decision* made the game unique because it allowed surrendering half your bet and giving up the hand before the dealer checked the hole card. It had a huge impact on the player's advantage because, on hands where the dealer had a blackjack, the player executing early surrender lost only half his bet to the dealer's strongest hand.

Julian Braun, who worked with a number of the pioneers of card counting systems, quickly developed a basic strategy for the new early-surrender decision, which yielded a player advantage of 0.25 percent off the top of their four-deck shoe games. I published this strategy in my gaming column in the *Philadelphia Inquirer* and the rush was on to get the money. Early surrender and the other regulation requiring the casinos to deal two-thirds of a shoe before shuffling attracted hordes of card counters to the "candy store," including the famed blackjack player Kenny Uston and his blackjack teams.

The fun lasted only until 1981, when casino management persuaded the New Jersey Casino Control Commission to eliminate these two rules and to give them the right to bar suspected card counters from play.

Uston sued over the barring issue and won his case in the New Jersey Supreme Court, but the game was changed forever. I described these changes and the problems they created in my book *Break the Dealer*, published in 1985.

The first change required the casinos to deal to everyone, including suspected card counters. The casinos countered this change by increasing the number of decks to eight and changing their wash and shuffle procedures; their objective in doing so was to introduce card clumping into the game. The *wash* is the procedure casinos use when new decks are introduced into play. Subtle and sophisticated methods were used to eliminate a random wash and introduce clumping into play. Read what Kenny Uston wrote about this wash in his blackjack newsletter:

> Caesar's shuffle at the beginning of each shift is devastating to the counter. Cards of similar denomination and suit tend to stay together. I lost about $15,000 on the first shoe of the day shift as I watched all the low cards dealt, followed by spades. I called over a Commission Official and had him observe the first shoe at another table. In the third round, of seven cards exposed, there was a royal flush in clubs. Card counting depends on the random ordering of the cards. Clumping such as this will obliterate the counter.

I wrote in *Break the Dealer* that "excessive clumping resulting from inadequately washed cards can be encouraged and prolonged by sophisticated shuffling procedures. These procedures have been incorporated in Nevada games since at least 1979. Atlantic City began to use them following the Uston court decision. Since then, shuffles have been continuously modified with the sole purpose of subverting mathematical systems used to gain an advantage in blackjack."

In the 1990 edition of *Blackjack: A Winner's Handbook,* I explained this phenomenon even more clearly by warning the card counter not to bet up into a rapidly rising count. The count is rising into a low-card clump, which are dealer-favorable cards; low cards can be devastating to the player.

This, then, is the problem in a nutshell: The 1 percent theoretical advantage in the multi-deck shoe game was nullified by the casinos with their wash and shuffle procedures for all but the most skilled card counters who were willing to play to the "long run." And the advantage achieved by these skilled counters is, in my opinion, only about ½ percent at best.

But did this stop the new breed of blackjack authors from continuing with their card counting studies and publishing their blackjack books and newsletters? No way. In fact, more books than ever were published in the 1980s. Blackjack newsletters flourished. Why did this happen if the advantage had essentially been nullified in the shoe games? Because these writers were selling a myth—the myth that card counting still worked in the shoe games.

Most of these blackjack authors were identified in the 1990 edition of my book *Blackjack: A Winner's Handbook*, so it is not necessary to review their work here. There is one author, however, whose work I have decided to discuss because he represents all the reasons why you should avoid card counting in the multi-deck shoe game. His name is Stuart Perry, and he self-published a book called *Las Vegas Blackjack Diary* in 1995. All of the comments that follow are my opinions based on over 40 years of blackjack play, instruction, and research.

If you could take every book and every newsletter that the card counters have written and stuff their contents into one blackjack player, Stuart Perry would be that person. In his book, he tells of spending many months and many hundreds of hours practicing card counting, both at home and in the casinos, getting ready for a big four-month trip to play serious blackjack in Las Vegas.

Backed by a $20,000 bankroll during the time he spent in Vegas, Stuart played 231 hours and won $2,303 or about $10 per hour. Stuart blamed his small win on bankroll fluctuations and on the fact that he did not play to the "long run." He estimates that 50,000 hands or more are needed to reach the long run and "in decent games."

Stuart is the only case study I need to support my claims about a card counting myth in the multi-deck shoe games. Here is a guy that played about as close to perfect as you can expect, and he ended up winning only $10 an hour on his "serious trip."

Does $10 per hour tempt you into wanting to learn how to count? Remember that Perry needed a $20,000 bankroll and many months of practice to achieve his small edge. But did he really have an edge in the multi-deck game? Let's continue our discussion.

An analysis of Stuart's data reveals that most of his wins came in single- and double-deck games, in which card counting works; many of his big losses came in the six-deck games, in which he laments about losing on the high counts. The following selected quotes indicate to me that Stuart was making the same mistake made by many counters who do not understand that card clumping in these games can obliterate their advantage:

"I lost a series of high-count bets to make the session a losing one."

"The count was steadily going up and I was losing most of the hands."

"[I] got slaughtered on two high-count shoes."

In the last shoe in this example, Stuart describes losing $800 in a high-count hand, including a double down to a dealer four-card 21 (an indicator of low-card clumping).

Do you see what's happening here? Stuart is betting up into low-card clumps producing a high-count hand (low cards are counted as +1), which is supposed to mean that the player has the advantage on the next hand. So Perry increases his bet in anticipation of the player-favorable high cards appearing on the next hand. But, because of low-card clumping, they don't come out when anticipated by the high-count. More low-cards equals big bet losses on high-count hands.

He could have realized a nice win by learning how to avoid those shoe games where low-card clumps produce false high-count hands. Or he could have avoided all shoe games and probably realized a nice win in the single- and double-deck games. If Stuart Perry would separate out the shoe games from his records, he would undoubtedly find that the single- and double-deck games produced a nice win for the eight-week period he was in Vegas, probably right around expected value.

Two other conclusions can be drawn from the Perry case study in assessing today's state of the art in blackjack advantage systems.

The first is the difficulty in using card counting to play blackjack professionally. Perry was barred from play at least four times. His exposure was high in casinos where he was winning, and he wasn't skilled enough to camouflage his play. But few players are skilled enough under today's tough conditions to make a living off the single- and double-deck tables.

The second conclusion that can be drawn from the Perry case study concerns using the count to play the hands. Perry himself reaches the conclusion that "the calculations that must be made at casino speed can be mentally draining."

My question is, for whom? For what? What is the benefit of spending hundreds of hours learning point-count index tables for playing the hands according to the count? The card counters tell you that it's about one quarter of 1 percent of additional advantage. But this figure is from their theoretical studies, which they have been working on and fine tuning since Stanford Wong published his version of them in the late 1970s. This theoretical quarter percent and what it means to the card counters is much of what drives their newsletter and book industry, where these guys make their money.

For all but the most skilled counters, this quarter percent evaporates under the heat of casino play—either through mental calculation errors or through camouflaging one's play to avoid being detected as a counter. So the myth is perpetuated and the recreational gambler who learns card counting continues to mistakenly believe that he or she has an advantage over the casino.

So this, dear reader, is the sad state of the art in card counting systems as we enter a new millennium.

My overall conclusion: Stay away from card counting in the multi-deck shoe game. Now, let's review the alternative and turn to that second question I raised at the beginning of this chapter: Does the non-random shuffle create exploitable player biases in the multi-deck shoe game? The following discussion lays the groundwork for the answer to this question, which is discussed in Chapter 5.

THE EFFECT OF THE NON-RANDOM SHUFFLE IN THE MULTI-DECK SHOE GAME

In the introduction to this book, we introduced the notion of non-randomness. Scientists claim that nothing in this universe is really random, ergo everything must be predictable. Let's apply this notion to blackjack.

In January 1990, the *New York Times* published an article by Gina Kolata describing the results of a major study on card shuffles. The study, conducted by Dr. Persi Diaconis, a Harvard mathematician, proved conclusively that it takes seven shuffles to obtain randomness in a single deck of cards. In describing the study results, Ms. Kolata wrote, "The realization that most shuffled decks are not actually random allows gamblers to improve their odds of winning." She went on to quote Dr. Diaconis: "There are people who go to the casino and make money on this," he said. "I know people who are out there doing that now." Diaconis may have been referring to my students and me, because we had known about this phenomenon for almost a decade prior to the publication of his study.

Most of our research was aimed at detecting biases in the shoe game because, even if the dealer shuffled seven times (and few, if any, do), with the extra decks it was still insufficient to obtain a random game.

As documented in *Break the Dealer* and *Blackjack: A Winner's Handbook*, I was the first blackjack expert to deviate from accepted card counting theory and go in a different direction—looking for the non-randomness in casino blackjack and ways in which it could be exploited.

We developed a method called TARGET 21, the essence of which is scouting for winning tables that exhibit biases created by the non-random shuffle and that the player can exploit.

The scouting process for these player-favorable games is based on 21 carefully researched and validated factors. In the 1990 edition of *Blackjack: A Winner's Handbook*, I published a few of these factors. My objective was to give the reader something he or she could use to prove that biases exist and confirm that they can be exploited. Judging by reader response, this objective was more than fulfilled.

Chapter 7 of this book contains the advantage method, which is based on the TARGET 21 method, in the section titled "Blackjack's Winning Factors." This method can be employed in the casino with very little practice. If you're a card counter, I urge you to compare its performance with whatever count system you're using.

Additional information on the complete TARGET 21 home study course and other blackjack courses can be obtained by contacting me using the form at the back of this book.

THE STATE OF THE ART IN SINGLE- AND DOUBLE-DECK BLACKJACK ADVANTAGE SYSTEMS

You can still beat the single- and double-deck games with card counting using the High-Low Point Count System. You won't get a complete deck or 51 cards dealt to you, as the casinos did in the old days, but you will get two-thirds of a deck or two-thirds of two decks dealt in many casinos.

Most handheld games, as single- and double-deck games are called, are found in Nevada casinos. A few are offered in the Southern Mississippi casinos, and once in a while a handheld game will pop up elsewhere.

The current state of the art is several point-count systems—one-level, two-level, and three-level. Some of these, such as High-Opt I and II, require a side count of aces. All come with tables of indexes for use in modifying the basic strategy.

If you play the handheld games, I urge you to stay with the simple High-Low Point Count System. If you learn any of the index numbers for modifying the hand based on the count, I suggest you stay in the range of −1, 0, +1 to keep it simple.

But card counting alone is not enough to fully exploit the benefits offered by single- and double-deck games. A method for combining the best of both worlds—card counting and bias exploitation caused by the non-random shuffle—is presented in Chapter 8, "Advantage Blackjack for Single- and Double-Deck (Handheld) Games."

Five

Exploitable Biases in Multi-Deck Blackjack Games

The purpose of this chapter is to document a definitive answer to the following question: Does the non-random shuffle create exploitable player biases in a multi-deck shoe game? This answer will lay the groundwork for the advantage system discussed in Chapter 7. In this chapter you will learn:

- What a bias is in a blackjack game

- Player-favorable and dealer-favorable cards and card combinations and their impact on the player's hand

- Unequal distribution of player- and dealer-favorable cards and card combinations and their impact on the player

- What card clumping is and how it affects the game

- The influence of the dealer up-card on clumping and card sifting

- How the non-random shuffle preserves clumps from shoe to shoe and how this engenders player biases
- Why full tables produce dealer biases
- The influence of shuffles and shuffle procedures on card clumps: plugging, stripping, pick size, and intertwine
- Why dealer-breaking activity occurs

All of these have an impact on the blackjack game you are in; understanding these ideas should convince you that (1) blackjack is a non-random game and (2) if it is not random, it is predictable. The intent of this chapter is to provide a basis of understanding so you will be better armed to employ the advantage strategy described in Chapter 7.

WHAT IS A BIAS?

The American Heritage Dictionary of the English Language (Houghton Mifflin, 1992) defines a bias as "a statistical sampling or testing error caused by systematically favoring some outcomes over others."

A bias in blackjack is when the card distribution or pattern in a shoe is such that the true percent advantage deviates from the normal overall advantage a casino enjoys in a random game where the players are playing perfect basic strategy.

Advantage is the average amount of money won divided by the total amount of money bet. For example, if a casino enjoys a 1 percent advantage, then the casino expects to make $1 for every $100 bet (1 percent × $100).

As you may know, the casino *hold percentage* (the percent of player buy-ins left behind by the players, or percent losses) is consistently much higher than the casino's theoretical advantage in all casino games. Most of this discrepancy is probably due to players overbetting their bankrolls and tapping out. Some of it is due to poor play decisions by the players. The average player probably gives up about 4–6 percent by poor play.

Above and beyond these factors, some of this discrepancy is due to non-random card distribution and patterns that occur as a result of random drift, casino shuffles, and the sorting of the cards by normal dealing, player hitting, standing, breaking, and dealer card pickup procedures. Most of the non-random card patterns that develop favor the casino. Many of the casino shuffles not only will tend to preserve a dealer bias, but may even enhance or help create dealer biases, especially in full tables. Other casino shuffles tend to preserve either bias — dealer or player. Since the normal sorting of the cards during dealing and playing usually favors the formation of dealer biases, and because the casino enjoys a theoretical advantage overall, dealer biases are the most common type of bias.

PLAYER- AND DEALER-FAVORABLE CARDS AND COMBINATIONS

Computer studies have determined individual player-favorable and dealer-favorable cards by removing a card value from a deck and determining the effect of its removal on the player or dealer advantage. From these studies, it was determined that the effect of removing 2, 3, 4, 5, 6, and to a small extent 7, are player favorable, and the 9, 10, and ace are dealer favorable. Eight was determined to be neutral. Essentially, with the exception of the dealer ace, it is the ability of these cards to make or break the dealer's hand when he has a stiff that determines whether a card value is player favorable or dealer favorable. Since an ace can count as 1 or 11, it can behave as a low or high card and actually tends to reduce dealer breaking. It is a player-favorable card because blackjack pays 3 to 2. In fact, this 3-to-2 blackjack bonus adds about 2 percent advantage to the player over even-money blackjack.

Card counting systems assign index numbers to card values based on the approximate effects of the removal of these cards to allow a card counter to determine whether he has an advantage during the remainder of a shoe or deck. These systems can successfully determine when a player has an edge, especially in single- and double-deck games. Multi-deck shoes require a very large betting spread, back counting, or team play to be beaten. The information a counter gains is limited. He does not know the location of the player-favorable cards, only that there is a higher- or lower-than-normal ratio of player-favorable to dealer-favorable cards over the remainder of the shoe. He must "pay rent" during long periods of negative and neutral counts waiting for potentially advantageous situations to occur (if at all) near the end of the shoe.

Effects of Multiple Card Combinations

What we know about the effect of the removal of individual cards is valuable, but blackjack hands consist of two or more cards. Some card combinations favor the dealer and others favor the player. When the cards are first dealt, both players and dealers receive two cards. After viewing the first two cards, both must then decide whether to take one or more additional cards. Overall, the average number of cards in a blackjack hand is 2.8.

Because both players and dealers are initially dealt two cards that are possibly followed by one or more hit cards, we need to learn what card values combine to make strong or weak two-card hands and whether they then combine to form strong three-card hands. We can determine how cards combine by creating a matrix with card values heading the columns and rows and the sums of these card values in the body of the matrix.

Core Cards. The 5, 6, 7, and 8 card values are known as *core cards*, a concept developed by Scott Frank and outlined in his book *Blackjack for Winners* (Barricade Books, 1993). He has contributed much of what we know of the effects of multiple cards. We will expand on this concept and adapt it to the shoe game.

These core cards combine to form two-card hands that are mostly stiffs. The vast majority of two-card double-down opportunities include at least one of these cards but, when combined with another core card, form poor final hand totals. From the dealer's perspective, core cards usually combine well as three-card hands, resulting in fewer dealer breaks and strong dealer standing hands.

The remaining card values (ace, 2–4, 9, 10) combine to make many strong two-card hands such as 19, 20, and blackjack. When a player has a double-down opportunity, he is likely to draw a good hit card. From the dealer's perspective, hitting two-card stiffs will be less successful. Most of the time he will break or not "complete" his hand and will have to hit again.

When a region of the shoe is relatively high in core cards, there will be less overall breaking; fewer blackjacks; more two-card hands of 15–18; more double-down opportunities (but with bad hits); more successful hits on 12s, 13s, and 14s; and more dealer standing hands. Most player losses will be by stiffs left standing or by standing hands one or two points lower than the dealer. The game will appear slow and laborious because of the many decision hands.

Dealer Bias. When the majority of rounds in a shoe contain a high proportion of core cards, a strong dealer bias exists. This condition is often the result of 10s being concentrated into small areas of the shoe. Tens will appear to come out in many small concentrated clumps or a few large clumps.

If core cards become clumped together in a small area of the shoe, as the 10s were in the preceding example, a player bias will exist. The majority of rounds will be relatively depleted of core cards. There will be a relatively higher proportion of 10s, 20s, and blackjacks; fewer double-down opportunities (but with better hits); less successful hits on 12s, 13s, and 14s; and more dealer breaks on stiffs. Most player losses will be by breaking or by standing hands two or more points lower than the dealer.

Like-value cards tend to clump together due to the play of the game and casino shuffles. For this reason, it is not unusual for clumps of two or more core cards to occur, because core cards are consecutive in value. The same is true for high-value cards (9s and 10s) and low-value cards (2s–4s). The types of unequal distributions described in the previous examples affect overall player winning and losing. The types of distributions where one, two, or more dealer-favorable cards clump out of play result in overall player winning at a table. Winning factors draw attention to themselves and can be detected by the astute player.

While you are scouting a table and confirming the presence of winning factors, observe the overall distribution of card values. If the game is favorable to the player, there will seem to be plenty of 10s scattered around the table. Aces may also seem to be plentiful. If you see double-down hands, the players will usually be drawing 10s to them. While it is more difficult to notice when something is missing, try to see whether there are fewer-than-normal core cards. With normal distribution, they should make up a little less than a third of the cards. If there are fewer than in a normal distribution, there will often be fewer than the number of hands dealt. For example, with three player hands and one dealer hand, you will tend to see fewer than four core cards per round.

In a dealer-favorable game, the 10s will seem to be fewer than normal (less than the number of hands dealt). Double-down hands will seem to draw poor cards. If you are observing a table that exhibits this type of distribution, the player bias has deteriorated and players will soon be losing. Conversely, you may have just happened to walk up and observe a dealer-favorable clump of core cards. If the latter is true, it will not last more than two or three rounds. Wait and observe an extra round or two. If it continues, walk away. The player bias is no longer present. If the player winning improves and the dealer-favorable clump has passed, enter the game and follow betting, playing, and departure methods as discussed in later chapters.

CARD CLUMPING

So far, we have been describing the clumping of core cards or 10s into a concentrated area or a few areas of the shoe, leaving a majority of the rounds played deficient in those cards. We use winning factors (defined in Chapter 7) to find games where core cards and/or low cards are clumped out of play.

But this is not the only type of clumping that exists in today's games. Over a whole shoe, there can be an overall increase or decrease in density of various important card values, such as 10s and core cards. Overlaid on this long wave density can be short clumps of predominantly high cards, predominantly low cards, and alternating high and low cards. Typically, these short wave clumps can range from 4 to 12 cards long. Sometimes they can be consistent enough to gain useful information upon which to base betting and playing decisions.

Clumps of recognizable card patterns are stacked in the discard tray by the play of the hands and dealer card pickup procedures. Blackjacks and busted hands are usually picked up right away and placed in the discard tray. Multiple busted hands picked up in each round are called "break-card clumps." They consist mainly of a mixture of high and low cards.

The cards remaining on the table are nonbusted players' and dealer's hands. Frequently, these hands consist of a high proportion of two-card 19s and 20s. When this group of cards is placed in the discard tray, they frequently contain solid high-card clumps. This is the main reason high cards, especially 10s, are more likely than other cards to form solid clumps and become concentrated into small areas of the shoe. *This is an important concept in your understanding of clumping*. These high-card clumps exist and the nonrandom shuffle contributes to their perpetuation into the next shoe.

Influence of the Dealer Up-Card

The dealer's up-card affects player hitting and standing decisions.

High Up-Card. In the previous section, a high dealer up-card was shown to cause a tendency for 10s to clump. If the dealer shows a high up-card in a high percentage of rounds in a shoe, 10s will tend to become concentrated into solid clumps in the next shoe—a dealer-favorable situation. Not only will players tend to be losing, they will tend to lose in the next shoe. A relatively rare exception to this is if all the players have stiffs and break. In this case, the 10s are not sifted into solid clumps but form a large break-card clump.

Low Up-Card. If the dealer has a low up-card, the players will rarely take a hit that will break them. If no players break, 10-value cards will not tend to become concentrated into solid clumps because all the player hands will stay on the table until the end of the round. The mix of hands will generally be two-card stiffs and two-card pat hands. If the dealer has a low up-card, the 10s will tend to end up well distributed and in relatively high proportions in the discard tray after this type of round. If the dealer shows a low up-card in a majority of rounds in a shoe, not only will the players tend to be winning, but clumps of 10s will tend to be broken up and become well distributed in the next shoe, a player-favorable situation.

Preservation of Clumps from Shoe to Shoe

Individual cards are shuffled only about two or three times in most casino shuffles that are used in shoe games. For example, during a shuffle, the dealer may break a six-deck shoe in half, then take half-deck picks from each pile, riffle them three times, and repeat this until all the cards are shuffled. Each card is shuffled three times within a one-deck region of the shoe. Or a casino might use a *stutter* shuffle followed by a *perfect* (or *straight-through*) shuffle. With this type of shuffle, each card is shuffled two and a half times. Most individual cards do not move very much when subjected to a casino shuffle. For more on standard casino shuffles, see my book *Break the Dealer*.

Card values can be effectively grouped into categories such as high/low; high, core, and low; or player favorable and dealer favorable. As described earlier, these card categories tend to "clump up" and usually don't change very much from shoe to shoe. For example, when a significant portion of 10s becomes concentrated in a small area of the shoe, a single casino shuffle usually doesn't redistribute those 10s very much. It usually takes at least two or three shuffles. If card sorting by the dealer up-cards and play of the game, number of players, and so on is creating clumps of 10s, then this dealer bias can last indefinitely, since the low up-card type of clumping occurs less frequently and usually deteriorates after a relatively short time. But it can last two or three shoes and sometimes longer.

Full Tables and Dealer Biases

When the tables are full, the normal dealing of the rounds, player breaking, card pickup methods, and casino shuffles tend to produce strong dealer biases for a sustained period of time. In full tables, rounds frequently occur where a significant number of players hit and break while a significant number of others have two-card pat hands of 19 and 20. This tends to produce and sustain conditions where a significant number of 10s are rendered useless to the players in the majority of rounds by their concentration into small solid clumps. From the many "seed" clumps of solid 10s, many casino shuffles tend to create and maintain clumps of predominantly high cards and clumps of predominantly low cards that are about six to eight cards long. Often, you find sequences of high card, low card, high card, low card, and so on that are created when high- and low-card clumps are partially intertwined during the shuffle. These alternating high-card/low-card clumps are primarily located where a high clump changes to a low clump.

With random cards, the average number of two-card stiffs is about 38.5 percent. With clumps that are six to eight cards long and seven to eight hands per round at full tables, the conditions are ideal to produce many stiff hands, frequently exceeding 50 percent. It doesn't matter what up-card the dealer is showing because when a player has a stiff, he is always at a disadvantage. He is going to lose more of those hands than he wins no matter what up-card the dealer is showing.

If crowded conditions cannot be avoided, advanced playing and betting strategies must be employed. These include patient observation and disciplined play and carefully selecting where player-favorable rounds or areas of the shoe can be predicted and exploited.

Influence of Shuffle Procedures on Card Clumps

Most of the elaborate casino shuffles were probably originally developed to foil shuffle trackers. Some shuffles can be tracked, and we can predetermine where clumped regions in the discard tray will end up after a shuffle, either to predict where we will encounter the clump in the new shoe or to cut the clump into or out of play. My book *Blackjack: A Winner's Handbook* contains a chapter on shuffle tracking that tells you how to do this once very secretive technique.

Casinos don't always use elaborate shuffling procedures. Most casinos would prefer not to use them because they are time consuming. A growing number of casinos, at least in Las Vegas, are realizing that they lose far more money from lost playing time than they do from a few shuffle trackers, so they are using a short, simple shuffle. Players would rather play than watch someone go through an elaborate shuffle. They often get up and leave. The casino should also realize that it doesn't need to create and maintain dealer biases to make money. If players are consistently and rapidly mowed down by strong dealer biases, they will play somewhere else or quit playing entirely.

Plugging. *Plugging* is when the dealer takes segments (usually half-deck segments) of the unplayed cards that were behind the cut card and inserts them into the stack of cards in the discard tray. He may insert them randomly or in predetermined areas such as the bottom third, middle third, or top third of the one and a half decks that were behind the cut card. Plugging was originally used to foil shuffle trackers, but it also has the effect of shearing off like-card clumps to limit the size of those clumps. It can aid in maintaining short-clump dealer biases in full tables.

Stripping. *Stripping* is when the dealer takes usually about a deck of cards in one hand and "strips" off a small number of cards, letting them fall to the table. He may alternate taking a small number of cards from the top and bottom of the deck. If he takes a very small number of cards just off the top, it reverses the order of the cards in that deck and has a minimal effect on card clumps, at least within that deck. The top and bottom strip can break up clumps and may break up a bias. These strips are often used in single- and double-deck games to break up a possible bias when players are winning. A variation that can help maintain short-clump biases at full tables in shoe games is a "mild" strip, where the dealer combines each pair of half-deck picks and strips them four times by taking quarter-deck segments off the top. This has the effect of shearing off clumps and creating clumps that are six to eight cards long.

Stripping does not always break up player biases, but, generally, biases tend to be shorter at casinos where stripping is used.

Pick Size, Intertwine, and "Zippers." *Pick size* refers to the number of cards "picked" by the dealer as he goes through the shuffle process. Small pick size can limit the length of clumps and contribute to short-clumped dealer-biased games during crowded conditions.

Intertwine is also part of the shuffle process. It's concerned with how the cards are "laced" together as the dealer shuffles two clumps together. The tightest intertwine would be one card from each hand alternating as the two clumps are shuffled together.

Zippers are alternating high and low cards, such as K, 3, J, 5, 10, 4, and so on. A tight intertwine, which can be common among but not necessarily limited to relatively inexperienced dealers, can create a lot of zippers that result from the shuffling of a high-card clump into a low-card clump. These zippers frequently appear as transition zones between high-card and low-card clumps. These games can often be easy to "read" although not necessarily easy to beat.

How to Prove That Like-Card Clumping and a Non-Random Shuffle Exist

Take six or eight decks of fresh cards. Mark the vertical edges of each high card—9s, 10s, and face cards (not the aces)—with an indelible black felt-tip marker. Now thoroughly shuffle the cards (using a typical casino shuffle of your choice), and cut and place them in a shoe. Next, assume the position of the dealer and deal the entire shoe to six or seven phantom players. Play the players' hands using any strategy you choose. Be certain to pick up the cards and place them in the discard tray precisely the way it is done in the casino—break hands as they occur, standing hands at the end of the round. At the end of each shoe, shuffle, cut, and start again.

Do this for six or eight shoes, then place the decks on edge. You will start to see the marked cards and unmarked cards clump together. After a few more shoes, the decks on edge will start to resemble a product code label. That's how tight the clumps can become. Seeing is believing!

CONCLUSION

Our objectives will be to find and exploit player biases, to adapt our betting and playing strategies to beat weak dealer biases, and to avoid strong dealer biases. Our main goal will be to find player-biased games where dealer-favorable cards are clumped together in small areas of the shoe. In these games, player-favorable rounds will outnumber dealer-favorable rounds. With this information alone we can play with an advantage over the casino, and a strategy for doing so, in the section titled "Blackjack's Winning Factors," is presented in Chapter 7. Using this system, you will be able to find and exploit dealer-breaking tables and other player-favorable games.

But before I can teach you how to find and exploit player-favorable games, I would like to present a statistical analysis of dealer-breaking tables in the next chapter—irrefutable proof that they exist. Armed with this information, you will be ready and motivated to learn the advantage method presented in Chapter 7. Although the statistical data is described in simple terms and should be easy for you to understand, if you're not interested in the calculations and want to get right to the winning method, turn to Chapter 7.

Six

DEALER-BREAKING AND PLAYER-FAVORABLE GAMES

Most blackjack players at one time or another will admit to seeing a hot blackjack table where the dealer is breaking hand after hand and the players are raking in the chips. Even most card counters will admit to observing or participating in these kinds of games, although they claim there is no reason for them and that you can't predict them. But not only can you predict them, you can find them! Before I show you how, let me prove that they exist.

In Peter Griffin's book *The Theory of Blackjack* (Huntington Press, 1988) he states that the average dealer break percentage is 28 percent, meaning that, on average, the dealer breaks 28 times out of every 100 hands played. Just knowing this average doesn't help, because there are times when the dealer is breaking at a higher percentage and other times at a lower percentage. Clearly, we are most interested in games where the dealer is consistently breaking. The analysis in this chapter provides insight on how frequently one could expect higher dealer-breaking activity. I will use the standard deviation (a statistical measure of variability) to assess the variation of dealer breaks in a typical blackjack game. Don't let this term scare you because I'll walk you through, in simple terms, each step of the calculations and conclusions.

Because there can be two and only two possible outcomes for the dealer's hand, a standing hand of 17–21 or a break, a series of blackjack hands is a binomial probability distribution with a simple formula for calculating the standard deviation. Knowing the standard deviation tells us how often to expect the dealer to break more or less than the norm of 28 percent.

Our discussion will be based on a sample size of 100 hands. The standard deviation of 100 hands played is easily computed as follows:

n = number of hands played (100)

p = probability of a break (.28)

s = standard deviation

SQRT = square root

$s = \text{SQRT } (n \times p(1 - p))$

$s = \text{SQRT } (100 \times 0.28(1-.28))$

$s = \text{SQRT } (28 \times 0.72)$

$s = \text{SQRT}(20.16)$

$s = 4.5$

Therefore, the standard deviation is 4.5 hands in 100, or 4.5 percent. This means that for one standard deviation of 4.5 hands, the dealer breaks could be as high as 32.5 (28 + 4.5) or as few as 23.5 (28 − 4.5) in this 100-hand sample. The calculation for a number of hands other than 100 will yield a different number, but this number, 4.5, will suffice for our purposes.

Basic statistics tells us that, as shown in Figure 2, the dealer-breaking activity will be in the range of one standard deviation 68 percent of the time, in the range of two standard deviations 95 percent of the time, and in the range of three standard deviations 99.7 percent of the time.

Let's put these percentages in simple terms, remembering that 28 breaks per 100 hands is our average or norm. Dealer breaks fall

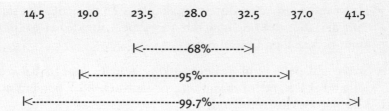

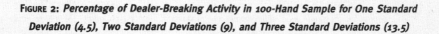

FIGURE 2: *Percentage of Dealer-Breaking Activity in 100-Hand Sample for One Standard Deviation (4.5), Two Standard Deviations (9), and Three Standard Deviations (13.5)*

within one standard deviation 68 percent of the time; this means that dealer breaks for our 100-hand sample will vary between 23.5 (28 − 4.5) and 32.5 (28 + 4.5) 68 percent of the time. Dealer breaks fall within two standard deviations 95 percent of the time; this means that the dealer breaks for our 100-hand sample will vary between 19 (28 − 9, or 4.5 times 2) and 37 (28 + 9, or 4.5 times 2) 95 percent of the time. Dealer breaks fall within three standard deviations 99.7 percent of the time; this means that dealer breaks for our 100-hand sample will vary between 14.5 and 41.5 breaks 99.7 percent of the time.

Using these laws of statistics, we now can show this graphically, as shown in Figure 2. Knowing now that for one standard deviation, or 68 percent of the time, the dealer will break between 23.5 and 32.5 times, what we are interested in is the other 32 percent. What happens in the lower 16 percent and the higher 16 percent? We're not interested in the 16 percent that represents the low end of the chart—only the 16 percent that represents the high end, where dealer breaking occurs more frequently.

Now let's lay our 100-hand sample on a casino with 100 tables; the logic is the same. Dealers at 68 tables would be breaking in the one-standard-deviation range, or between 23.5 and 32.5 times. But, on the high end, 16 tables could be outside this range—with the dealer-breaking average greater than 32.5 percent. Let's sum up before drawing conclusions.

- The average expected dealer break rate is 28 percent. The standard deviation tells us how often to expect the dealer to break more or less than this amount.

- Sixty-eight percent of dealer-breaking activity appears between −1 and +1 standard deviations, or between 23.5 percent and 32.5 percent for 100 hands.

- Ninety-five percent of all dealer-breaking activity appears between −2 and +2 standard deviations, or between 19 percent and 37 percent for 100 hands.

- Ninety-nine and seven-tenths percent of all dealer-breaking activity appears between −3 and +3 standard deviations, or between 14.5 percent and 41.5 percent for 100 hands.

The most important point to remember is that almost anything can happen in a small sample, and that's really what we are confronting as we approach and play any blackjack table.

Let's apply these statistics to the percentages of tables in a casino. For example, a casino with 100 tables could be expected to have 16 tables (16 percent) currently exhibiting dealer-breaking activity in the range of one standard deviation or more. We get the 16 percent by subtracting off the 68 percent of tables that are within the boundary of 68 percent and dividing by 2. We take the 16 percent of tables at the high end and ignore the other 16 percent at the low end.

Also using these statistics, we can easily determine that clearly 50 percent of the tables, 50 in this casino with 100 tables, will be dealer biased with an additional 34 percent, or 34 tables, dealer-biased but less so. This is illustrated in Figure 3.

These statistics verify that dealer-breaking and player-favorable games exist. If we use one standard deviation as the cutoff for playable games, then fully 16 percent of the tables should be playable. However, the strongest games, and thus the most profitable, will be confined to only about 2.5 percent of available tables — the higher end of the two standard deviations encompassing 95 percent of all tables.

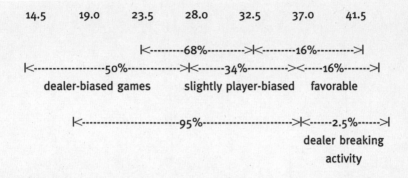

FIGURE 3: *Player-Favorable and -Unfavorable Games Based on Standard Deviation*

These numbers conform very closely to the empirical evidence collected over 15 years by thousands of players who use my methods.

So even though it would be quite difficult to mathematically calculate the precise dealer break percentage that gives the player an advantage, the empirical evidence and my 40 years of experience tell me that, as we approach and pass +1 standard deviation, we are entering a player-biased game that grows stronger as we reach +2 standard deviations—a definite advantage game! When a game exhibits dealer-breaking activity approaching +3 standard deviations, then we are entering the realm of a dealer-breaking home run table.

The table selection method given in "Blackjack's Winning Factors" in the next chapter will lead you to dealer-breaking and player-favorable games! Let's get to it.

Seven

ADVANTAGE BLACKJACK FOR MULTI-DECK SHOE GAMES

BLACKJACK'S WINNING FACTORS

Dealer-breaking tables and player-favorable games exhibit evidence of winning. This evidence can be quantified as factors—factors that point to winning tables. In this chapter, I will describe those factors for definition and description, which are key to establishing and maintaining an advantage over the dealer.

The Chip Factor

When looking for a playable game, look at the chips in front of the players. Learn how to identify the average buy-in sizes. If the players appear to have more chips in front of them than the average buy-in, you are looking at a game where players have probably been winning.

In evaluating players' chips for winning activity, use 20 times the table minimum as a guide. In a $5 table, if a player has more than $100 in front of him, there is a good chance that he is a winner. Also, look at the chips in the dealer's tray. If there are a lot of chips missing, make sure that the amount of chips in front of the players roughly matches the amount missing from the tray. That is a sign that the chips have been won at that table. If the amount of players' chips is much less than the amount missing from the dealer's tray, the chips may have been won or bought and taken away. Learning how to pay attention to what is happening with the chips on the table will help you find winning games.

The Game Factor

The game factor is the key to finding winning tables. Here you are looking for signs that the game has what we will call "integrity." This means, essentially, that the game is going our way. Look for a game where the majority of the players are making their hands, where the dealer is breaking often, and where the dealer is not getting a lot of 10-value cards or aces. Where you see this, you are looking at a game with good integrity.

Look for games where the players are betting more aggressively, putting out money for double downs and splits without deliberation. This indicates that the players have been winning and expect to win more. Where you see players deliberating over their bet decisions, passing up chances to double down or split their hands, these are signs that the game is going badly and should be passed over.

The Player Factor

Talk to players at the tables you are evaluating. Getting information from the players is vital to finding winning tables. You want to find out if there is winning activity at this table right now! Don't be afraid to talk to players—most people are more than happy to tell you how they are doing. Just be specific in the questions you ask. Don't just ask, "How's it going here?" You will get an equally general "Okay," or "Not so good." Instead, the more specific you are, the more specific the information you will get back. Ask questions such as, "Did the dealer break any of the last four or five hands?" While looking at the chips in front of the players, you might ask them how much they bought into the game for. Ask whether the players have been making their splits and double-down plays the last three to five hands. The information you will gain will be valuable and will help you decide whether the table is playable.

The Dealer Factor

The dealer is an important element of finding favorable games. Talk to the dealers when you are looking for good games. Often the dealers will tell you whether they have been beating the players or not. A dealer's job is often boring, and they are grateful for players who are pleasant and interesting and who help make the game interesting. Keeping a dealer's attitude in your favor can mean a more even game, with less variation in the shuffle and the chance of keeping a good game going longer.

BETTING TACTICS

Let's start by defining a betting unit based on bankroll size. Conservative players should establish a 100-unit bankroll and a betting unit of 1 percent of bankroll. For example, with a $1,000 bankroll your betting unit is $10. Aggressive players should not bet more than 2 percent of bankroll.

After you have found and entered a game exhibiting blackjack's winning factors, you must decide how to play and bet each hand. Playing the hand will be addressed in the next section. Here we are concerned with betting and we start by addressing the question of risk—do you want to bet aggressively or conservatively? Take your choice of betting strategy in each category. Let's start with conservative betting.

A Basic Betting Strategy

The conservative betting strategy I recommend is selected from the TARGET 21 course and has been successfully used by thousands of players since the early 1980s.

It consists of flat-betting your hand until you have won three more hands than you have lost. For example, you enter a $5 game, bet $10 per hand (your betting unit), and win three more hands than you lose. Now you are $30 ahead and have a decision to make: raising or lowering your bet or keeping it the same. Here are your options for making this decision:

Option 1. If the game factor is strong, you should consider raising your bet (I'll discuss the amount of the raise in a moment).

Option 2. If you're uncertain about the strength of the game, and your goal is to depart this table with a win, consider keeping your bet the same and setting a tight two-unit stop-loss that would trigger a table departure.

Option 3. If you're a conservative bettor, reduce your bet to $5 (assuming a $5 minimum table) and set a three-unit stop-loss for departing this table.

If you raise your bet in a strong table (option 1), I suggest no more than 25 percent, rounding up or down to the nearest dollar amount (for example, if you have been betting $10, raise your bet to either $12 or $13). If the game continues strong, raise your bet each time you win another three units. Set a three-unit stop-loss.

If you elect option 2 and continue to win, use a trailing stop-loss of three units. For example, if you find yourself four or more units ahead in this game, move your stop-loss up as you continue to win. With a four-unit win, your trailing stop-loss is now three units and you have essentially locked up one unit of profit (a *win-lock*) for this game. As your win level continues to increase, your win-lock increases; a five-unit win yields a win-lock of two units, a six-unit win yields a win-lock of three units and so forth.

If the game becomes very strong, the dealer starts breaking like crazy, and the players are winning, you might be strongly tempted to increase your bet size. But before you do, understand that you can win with flat-betting in qualified games. There is nothing wrong with staying at the same betting level the entire time you're at the table. Many of my students and instructors have flat-bet their way to a $10,000 bankroll with $25 units. To repeat, you can win by flat-betting because you'll win more hands than you'll lose in games qualified by blackjack's winning factors. Not in every game, mind you. That is why we establish and follow solid money management discipline as described in the following pages. The idea is to get away from bad games quickly, cut your losses short, and let your profits accumulate in good games.

Whether you should increase your bet pertains to both options 2 and 3. First of all, your objective is to get out of this game with winnings. In most games, player biases do not last that long. If you stay too long, you make the transition from playing to gambling. Your advantage is dissipated. If you want to become an advantage player, play when the advantage is working for you; when it reverts to the dealer, find another game.

In games where your advantage sustains over a number of shoes, the money management techniques that follow will keep you in the game to optimize your win. Follow my recommendations for stop-losses and win-locks and you will "get the money."

An Aggressive Betting Strategy—Ride the Bias

You're in a strong game with the dealer breaking much more than 28 percent—maybe even a "home run" game with the dealer breaking 50 percent of the time in the last shoe or two. It's time to step up the betting. You can use this strategy when you first sit down, or you can move up to it after winning six units or more—it's your choice, depending on the degree of risk you wish to take.

The name "Ride the Bias" means to bet according to how the players in this game did on the last hand. For example, if there are five players in your game, and three won on the last hand (including you), bet the difference in units—three winning players minus two losing players equals a one-unit bet. If four players win, including you, and one loses, bet three units. If all five win on a dealer break, for example, bet five units on the next hand.

Money Management

You must define your *maximum* bet. It should not be more than five units, but it can be as few as two units. I suggest staying with a one-unit bet if you lose, no matter what the other players did on the prior round, but aggressive bettors may wish to bet up even on a loss.

I suggest a stop-loss point of six units. When you are down by six units, then it is time to go. This means that you could get forced out of this game after losing two hands in succession if you are betting three units on each hand.

The best way to bet in a strong game with Ride the Bias is to take your table stake of six units and divide it into three stacks of two units each. These stacks represent three bets of two units each. This is the way you start. If the game turns sour right away (you lose three bets in a row), you're out of the game. If you chop back and forth with these three bets over half to a full shoe, you can stay in the game or exit—your choice. You may wish to revert to the basic betting strategy described earlier.

But once you start winning, and in many games you will because you've qualified the table as a winning table with dealer-breaking activity, this is where the fun begins. Use your win to increase the size of the three stacks evenly, beginning with the leftmost stack (you're betting from the rightmost stack). So the stacks increase evenly, first to three chips then to four, five, and so on. As your stacks increase, your maximum bet increases, so now you can bet three units, for example, when three more players win than lose on the prior round.

Here is the way to increase your bet in a strong table using Ride the Bias. The numbers shown in Table 1 on page 79 represent $10 units and assume a betting unit of $10. For example, three units in the chip stacks would equate to six $5 chips. All numbers shown are units.

Units in Each Chip Stack (Total units in 3 chip stacks)	Maximum Bet in units	Stop-Loss in units	Win-Lock in units
3 (9)	2	6	3
4 (12)	2	6	6
5 (15)	3	9	6
6 (18)	3	9	9
7 (21)	4	12	9
8 (24)	4	12	12
9 (27)	5	15	12
10 (30)	5	15	15

TABLE 1: *Bet Sizing Using the Ride the Bias Betting Strategy*

Remember to keep the number of chips in each of the three stacks even. As the chip stacks begin to build, the conservative player may wish to take the two left stacks as the win-lock and use the right pile for betting. In this case, the maximum bet would obviously depend on the number of chips in the right stack. The line in Table 1 represents a possible conservative departure from the aggressive Ride the Bias. Beginning at level 6 (6 chips in each stack, with a total of 18 units), the conservative player would regress to a two-unit maximum bet, working off the right stack to make his bets with the left two piles "locked up." Once that right stack is gone, leave the table.

As you win hands, put your winning chips on the left two stacks first, then keep all stacks level. This conservative strategy may trigger a quicker departure, but you're taking more of your win with you on a lower level of departure.

Readers wanting additional betting tactics can refer to *Blackjack: A Winner's Handbook*, specifically the Takedown Strategy, a reader favorite.

A Risk-Averse Basic Strategy

Multi-deck blackjack is a game of non-random shuffles and biases. My instructors, my students, and I have long recognized that today's game is not the game that was in place when Cantey, Baldwin, Maisel, and McDermott invented the basic strategy in 1958. Nor is it the game that was in place when Braun modified the basic strategy in the 1970s. All of the findings of blackjack's pioneers were based on a game that no longer exists—a random game created by a computer.

You have learned in this chapter that card clumping affects your chances of winning and losing each hand, and therefore your chances of leaving each table a winner. Because of clumping and its effect on a player's hand, the traditional basic strategy needs to be overhauled.

My associates and I have developed a strategy we call Clump Card Strategy or CCS. CCS is a risk-averse strategy. Many double and split plays are devastating to the player. If you look at the math of the original basic strategy, 25 percent of all doubles and splits yield less than a 1 percent gain. Clumping virtually eliminates this gain, so when you double down or split on these plays for no real gain, you are courting disaster. There is no value, no gain, and no edge. So I am recommending that you become strongly disinclined or reluctant to make these plays—become risk averse!

CCS eliminates all doubles and splits that do not deliver a measurable advantage to the player. When using blackjack's winning factors to enter a qualified game, you are starting out even with the casino when using CCS. All doubles and splits listed here deliver a 10 percent player expectation of winning.

Here are the changes to the basic strategy for the six- and eight-deck shoe games, assuming you can double after splitting, you can resplit pairs, and the dealer stands on soft 17.

Double Downs

For a hand totaling 9, double down on a dealer up-card of 4–6, *not* 3–6.

For a hand totaling 10 or 11, double down on a dealer up-card of 2–8, *not* 2–9 or 2–10.

On A–5, double down on a dealer up-card of 6, *not* 4, 5, or 6.

On A–6, double down on a dealer up-card of 5 or 6, *not* 3, 4, 5, or 6.

On A–7, double down on a dealer up-card of 4, 5, or 6, *not* 3, 4, 5, or 6.

Do not double on A–2, A–3, and A–4.

Splits

Never split 2s, 3s, and 4s.

Split 6s on a dealer up-card of 5 or 6, *not* 3, 4, 5, or 6.

Split 8s on a dealer up-card of 2–8, *not* always; hit a pair of 8s on a dealer up-card of 9, 10, or A.

Split 9s on 4–6, *not* 2–9 except 7.

Hitting and Standing

If your hand totals 13, hit on an up-card of 2 instead of standing. For any A–7 or hand totaling soft 18, stand on 9, 10, or ace instead of hitting.

If the casino allows surrender, follow this strategy:

Surrender

Surrender 16 against a 10 or ace, including a pair of 8s; do not split the 8s as you would do using basic strategy; surrender 16 against a 9, including a pair of 8s.

Surrender 15 against a 10 or ace, including an 8–7; do not hit the 8–7 as you would do using basic strategy.

RECOMMENDATIONS FOR CARD COUNTERS

I recognize that not all card counters reading this book will jettison the count system in favor of using the winning factors. If you're in this category, I strongly urge you to integrate the winning factors with your count. Here's how:

- Do not bet up into a rapidly rising count; wait for a count reversal before you bet.

- Do not enter games where the majority of players are obviously losing.

- Do not play into new decks of cards; if you do, play extremely cautiously because of the heavy clumping.

- For reasons mentioned in Chapter 5, be extremely cautious when playing in full tables.

- Set a reasonable stop-loss for your game and leave when it's triggered, count or no count.

- Observe the game factor as you maintain the count. Use it as an early warning of deterioration and indicator of possible table departure — if you stay in deteriorating games, keep track of how much you lose or "give back" in these games (eventually, you may accept this recommendation and depart).

- Do not play at an open table. There are usually good reasons why all players have departed — heavy clumping. If you insist on playing in these games, keep track of your wins and losses. As your net losses mount, consider my recommendation about no play.

If you use the count to modify basic strategy, also consider using the risk-averse Clump Card Strategy, especially if you are betting up into a rapidly rising count.

For additional recommendations, see the section on Count Reversal Strategy in Chapter 15 of *Blackjack: A Winner's Handbook*.

ADVICE FOR RECREATIONAL PLAYERS

To use blackjack's winning factors and gain an advantage, you have to scout for tables and ensure they're qualified prior to entry. If you're gambling for fun and don't want to make this commitment of time and effort to become an advantage player, that's okay; it's your decision. But, I do urge you to use the betting strategies in this book. You can use them at any table you play. And, who knows, you might just luck into a dealer-breaking table and really clean up!

The shoe game is still the prevalent game in today's blackjack and probably always will be, to make it as difficult as possible for the card counter to get an advantage. But there is a throwback game that you can still beat by card counting—the handheld game (single-deck and double-deck blackjack), discussed in the next chapter.

Readers interested in further instruction about how to beat the shoe game should refer to the appendix, which introduces the TARGET 21 and Blackjack Masters home study courses available from the author.

Readers interested in getting involved with the instructional programs could start with the book *Blackjack: A Winner's Handbook*. It can be obtained through the information in the appendix.

Eight

ADVANTAGE BLACKJACK FOR SINGLE- AND DOUBLE-DECK (HANDHELD) GAMES

Single- and double-deck blackjack is back! With the explosion of casinos in this country, competition has become fierce. Casino management has learned that offering single- and double-deck blackjack games give them a competitive edge over other houses. The gambling public loves the single- and double-deck game and will often opt for those casinos offering it.

Since these games are dealt from the dealer's hand and not the shoe, they are termed *handheld games* and are referred to as such from this point forward.

Many Las Vegas casinos offer handheld blackjack, as do casinos in Reno, Lake Tahoe, and Laughlin, Nevada. Some Southern Mississippi casinos offer handheld blackjack, and Indian casinos are getting on the bandwagon. The trend is for casinos to offer at least a few tables featuring single- or double-deck, and we expect this trend to continue.

THE ADVANTAGES OF HANDHELD BLACKJACK

Before we get down to business, let's explain why the handheld game is blackjack's most popular (and most beatable) game, and how it differs from the now traditional six- or eight-deck shoe game.

Dealing from a 52-card deck (or 104 cards in the double-deck game) improves your odds of being dealt a blackjack. Sure, it improves the dealer's odds, too, but remember you get paid 3 to 2 on the blackjack, and the dealer doesn't.

The 52- or 104-card deck also improves the mathematics of the game, which enables the player to make more aggressive plays, such as doubling down and splitting pairs more often, thus winning more money.

There is less clumping in a handheld game than in a shoe game. It has been proven that the shuffles are non-random, which causes more clumping in shoe games. More clumping can be unfavorable to the player. For example, if the 10s and aces clump together, many of them may be dealt out in successive rounds of play; thus they are out of play and not there when the player needs a 10 for a doubled 11 or to pair up with a first-card ace. Not so in the handheld game — it is more predictable. When you need a 10 for a doubled hand you are more likely to get one. When the dealer needs a 10 or face card to break his hand, he is more likely to draw one in the handheld game.

Card counting works for the handheld game because there is much less clumping to contend with. Your count, which indicates the high cards remaining to be played (or lack thereof), is a good betting tool and can also be used to modify basic strategy. More on this in a moment.

WINNING FACTORS FOR THE HANDHELD GAME

You have already learned blackjack's winning factors for the shoe game, most of which apply here. But to beat the handheld game, you must learn an additional, important factor — dealer *tokes*, or tips.

Dealer tokes take on immense importance in this game. If you see a stack of chips on the table by the dealer, usually behind the money slot in the table, or if you see the pocket of the dealer's vest bulging with chips, this is a *very* critical indicator that there is winning activity right now. For the handheld game, the tokes won by the dealer should be considered a "superfactor!" Here's why: Dealer tokes do not go into a box as in the shoe game; they stay on the table or go into the dealer's breast pocket. And when the dealer takes a break about every 40 minutes, the tokes go with him and are dropped into a drawer for later counting and splitting. This means that, on the average, this information is only about 20 minutes old! So it is a key indicator of player winning in this game. Use it with the other factors as the basis for table entry. The size and frequency of dealer tokes can be the sole basis for whether to enter a table in the handheld game.

Table Entry, Betting Tactics, and Departure

Once you make a decision to enter a game, buy in for no more than 10 betting units. Set a stop-loss of six units. Put a small betting pile of six units to one side. Bet from this pile. If you win, keep the pile at six units; put the other winnings to one side. If you lose, your bet comes from this small pile. If the pile is used up, you are off the table. If you are winning, once you are about nine units ahead, use the special stop-win technique described in Chapter 7. Divide your winnings into the three stacks and follow the procedure.

Use the Basic Betting Strategy in Chapter 7

Watch the game after you enter. Pay attention to the things that led you to the table in the first place. If you begin to see more 10s and face cards for the dealer up-card, consider leaving the game — unless you are still winning. If you see other players digging for more money, even if you are not down, consider leaving the game; the positive bias is either gone or going. Why stick around to lose?

In all cases, honor your stop-losses and your stop-wins. Don't let the casino get control of you—keep your discipline and remain a successful winner.

CARD COUNTING

The count is much more effective in handheld games and should be used by serious and recreational players alike. Counting is simple, because you only have to remember the running count for two to three rounds in the single-deck game and maybe seven to nine rounds in the double-deck games. If you have trouble remembering the count through that many rounds in the double-deck game, try it in the single-deck game first.

The High-Low Count

Use the High-Low Count. You do not need a multi-level count to beat this game. Here is all you need to get started:

In the High-Low System, count 2 through 6 as +1; 7 through 9 as zero; and 10s, face cards, and aces as −1.

Count the cards as you see them dealt to the players and then to the dealer. Keep a running count; run the count from round to round until the dealer shuffles, then start over. Count each player's down cards as they are turned over on player breaks or on payoffs to players' winning hands. Count the dealer's hole card when it is turned over and then count additional cards as they are dealt to the dealer's hand.

Bet the count in units up to a maximum of four units. If your running count is +3, bet three units on the next hand. Many card counters will not "jump" their bets for fear of being identified as a counter by the floor persons in the pit. If you have this fear, watch how the other players bet and that should dispel it. Many players routinely raise their bets from 2 to 4, 1 to 4, 2 to 8, and so on. So if you're betting one unit off the top of a newly shuffled deck, and the count jumps to four in the first round, bet four units on the next hand.

Monitor the count carefully. If the high cards are not coming out when the count is plus and this turns into a trend over three or more shuffles, consider table departure; you are playing into a dealer bias caused by the non-random shuffle.

PLAYING HEAD-TO-HEAD

Aggressive players can open up a game and play head-to-head against the dealer. There are two keys: (1) Evaluate the game factor in the first two to three hands with a table minimum bet; (2) use the game factor to evaluate the game for two to three hands, and if it is positive, move to your full betting unit.

I would agree to give the more aggressive players a little more leeway with a stop-loss if the game is strong—but no more than nine units; the rule here, then, is a six- to nine-unit stop-loss based on your judgment of the strength of the game. Conservative players should avoid these games and concentrate on finding playable games with other players present.

BASIC STRATEGY FOR THE SINGLE-DECK GAME

Do not use the Clump Card Strategy described in Chapter 7 in the handheld game; use standard basic strategy as shown in Exhibit 2, Chapter 3.

There are some differences between the Las Vegas single-deck basic strategy and the Las Vegas multi-deck shoe strategy.

Refer to Exhibit 2 once again and examine the basic strategy grid. Notice that you double down on an 11 against a dealer ace. This is because of the greater chance of getting a 10 or face card in the single-deck game. You will double down on an 8-value hand of 6, 2 and 5, 3 against a dealer 5 or 6, again because of the greater probabilities of the dealer breaking on these up-cards, as opposed to a shoe game. For the same reason you double down on a hand of A, 8 against a dealer 6.

Notice that with a pair of 7s, you will stand against a dealer 10. This is because, quite simply, you must assume that the dealer has a 10 in the hole and the only thing that will save you is another 7. The odds are astronomically high against your drawing that third 7 because two of them are in your hand. So you stand and hope for the best. If the game allows surrender, you would surrender this hand against a dealer 10.

Splitting and Doubling Down

Because of the greater probabilities of catching a high card in the single-deck game, you split pairs more often. You will make these pair-split hands more often in the single-deck game than in a shoe game. Study your basic strategy carefully. If you can't play basic strategy exactly, you will be giving the casino more of an advantage over you than is necessary.

If you are playing a double-deck game, use single-deck basic strategy with one exception: Double down on 11 against an ace only if your 11 is made up of a 6, 5 or a 7, 4; do not double if your 11 is 8, 3 or 9, 2.

AGGRESSIVE BETTING TACTICS

If you find yourself in a choppy game that goes something like win a hand, lose a hand, win two hands, lose a hand, win a hand, lose two hands, win a hand, and so on, consider using a simple 1–2–4 up-as-you-lose strategy. You should adopt this strategy if the choppy nature of the game continues over four dealer shuffles or more. What this means is that you start by betting one unit; if you win, you continue betting one unit. If you lose, you bet two units. If you lose again, you bet four units. The objective of the up-as-you-lose strategy is to recoup the units lost and make a one-unit profit.

After each win, revert to a one-unit bet and continue betting one unit after each winning hand.

If you lose three up-as-you-lose bets, leave the table. With this strategy, you are risking seven units to win one, but many choppy games will persist long enough for you to take down a decent profit before you get forced out.

You can evaluate this betting tactic before using it by simply noting the number of losing hands in succession in your next game if that game seems to be chopping back and forth between you and the dealer. How quickly did you lose the three in a row?

Having read these last four chapters on blackjack, you can see that my focus is on the most popular of the casino table games. Blackjack will always be the staple game of the advantage player. Players interested in instruction on the handheld game can contact me directly using the coupon in the back of the book.

Section Three

CRAPS

Nine

BASIC CRAPS

HISTORY

The casino game of craps evolved over thousands of years. It is inextricably interwoven with the development of humanity. Prehistoric cavemen cast six-sided bones called *astragalas* that came from the ankles of clove-footed animals. The mythology of ancient Egypt, Greece, and Rome relates how the gods amused themselves at dice, with the destiny of the world riding on the outcome. Dice have been found in the ruins of Pompeii and in the burial chambers of the Pyramids. The Pharaohs as well as the Romans rolled dice for amusement, divination, and judicial decision. When Julius Caesar defied the Roman Senate and led his victorious army across the Rubicon, he took his announcement from the vocabulary of the dice shooter: *Iacta alea est*, or "the die is cast."

Even in the age of chivalry, knights entertained themselves and their ladies with games of dice. Gaming schools and guilds flourished, although by then gambling was frowned on by the church and it was frequently prohibited in various regions. Then, as now, the nobility was exempted, and the laws were enforced against the lower classes, especially on working days.

Today's casino craps can be traced directly to the game of hazard, first played by English Crusaders during the siege of an Arabian castle in the 12th century. Tosses of 2, 3, or 12 were referred to as "crabs." By the early 1800s, when the game was introduced to America in the port city of New Orleans, *crabs* had become *craps* and the rules had nearly evolved to those used today. Spreading rapidly up the Mississippi with the riverboat gamblers, and across the country via Pullman-car sharks, craps quickly replaced faro as the most popular gambling game. John H. Win is credited with banking the first craps game permitting right and wrong betting, charging bettors a 5 percent commission. Shortly after, Win designed the Philadelphia Layout, very much like the craps layout of today. It included a Don't Pass Line, which eventually evolved into the Don't Pass Bar 12 line, and eliminated the 5 percent commission. This feature took the game out of the streets and into the casinos.

TODAY'S GAME

Craps is my favorite game. You can yell and shout and let it all hang out. There is camaraderie at the craps table found in no other casino game. Unlike blackjack, where a dealer deals the cards, or roulette, where the croupier spins the wheel, the craps player initiates the action by throwing the dice.

Although the house's edge can be reduced to less than 1 percent, it must prevail in the long run (this is without the controlled throw or *rhythm roll*, discussed in the next chapter). Yet players who understand the rules and procedures of the game—which bets are most favorable, which bets to avoid, how to recognize and capitalize on a winning streak, and when to quit—can have a great time and possibly make quite a bit of money.

Many people confess their complete ignorance of the casino game of craps. Some men, especially war veterans, played a street game of dice that is quite different from bank craps as played in the most casinos. In any case, the concept of craps is quite simple and easy to understand. The biggest problem in the casino is overcoming the idea that the game itself is complicated. Far from it. The stumbling blocks rest in the elaborate layout, the odds, the action, the barking of the stickmen, and the shouting of the players, especially during a hot hand. I will do my best to take away the bewilderment.

The Players

Let's start with the players, men and women, rank beginners and old-timers, some laughing and shouting, some quiet and grim. Although they are all crowded around the table together, craps is not a group game. All players bet against the house, and one player's decisions in no way affect those of the others. The number of players is limited only by the number of people who can squeeze around the table. If you can slip in sideways and get to the layout, go for it.

If you are going to play, you will need to bet with chips or checks. Chips are required for craps with no exception, for several reasons. First, the bankroll needed by a casino is a fraction of what would be required if all tables were stocked with cash. Second, the different colors of the chips simplify the dealer's job of paying winning bets. Finally, the possibility of theft is reduced since stolen chips must be subsequently converted into cash.

How much cash you convert depends on the minimum bet and other factors. Each craps table has a minimum-bet requirement. A sign is positioned next to the dealers on either end to indicate the table stakes. You can easily tell the stakes by the color of the sign. A white sign indicates a $2 or $3 minimum bet (very few of these low-minimum tables are found in today's casinos); a red sign indicates a $5 minimum (the most common); light brown or blue or a similar color indicates a $10 minimum; green indicates a $25 minimum; blue indicates a $50 minimum; and black indicates a $100 minimum. Maximums usually vary between $300 and $1,000, although top casinos will raise the maximums at the request of a high-rolling player.

Place some of your currency in front of the dealer and, so that it will not be mistaken for a bet, announce clearly, "Change, please." Don't try to hand the dealer your money. Drop it on the table. Dealers are not allowed to take money out of your hand, and they are not permitted to hand you your chips. The dealer will usually repeat "Change only," and hand the money to the *boxman*, who counts it and tells the dealer the amount. The dealer will then place the equivalent amount of chips on the table in front of you. Pick them up and immediately place the chips you are not betting in the chip grooves provided in the table railing directly in front of you. Never leave chips on the layout, as they may be considered a bet. Remember that dealers must pay off all previous winning wagers and will usually set up new bets before stopping to make change. If you think the dice will be thrown before you get your chips, clearly announce the size and type of the wager you are making; if the dealer acknowledges it, called *booking*, you have a bet—even before you get your chips.

Casino Crew

We have briefly mentioned a dealer and a boxman. They are part of a four- or five-person crew consisting of a *stickman*, two dealers, and one or two boxmen who operate the game for the amusement of the players and the benefit of the house. The stickman, who conducts the game, controls the dice with a hooked stick, hence his name. From a bowl in front of him, he pushes five or six dice to a player. If the player does not care to roll the dice, he points to the next player, who is then presented with the dice. The shooter selects any two die, but when he is holding the dice, they must always be kept in view of the stickman; if not, they will be called back and examined by the boxman, and the player will be offered new dice from the bowl. After the dice are thrown to the opposite end of the table, the result is announced by the stickman, usually accompanied by a colorful banter. The stickman controls the pace of the game and also acts as a barker by calling out all the proposition bets that can be made with him. These are the worst bets for the player and the best bets for the house, and they account for a substantial portion of the casino's winnings.

In addition to placing the *puck* on the shooter's number, making change, collecting losing bets, and paying off winning bets, the two dealers, who stand opposite the stickman at each end of the table, are expected to help beginning players. Expert dealers soon become familiar with each player's betting style, anticipating their play and frequently pointing out an overlooked bet. One or two boxmen, the ultimate authorities at the table, sit between the dealers, watching the dice, the chips, the money, the dealers, and the players at all times.

The shooter is expected to toss the dice hard enough so they hit the backboard at the other end of the table. Although the throw is still considered legal if one or both dice fail to reach the end of the table, the boxman will strongly urge the shooter to throw harder. If a die bounces off the table or lands on a stack of chips or in the dice cup, the stickman announces, "No roll!" and the misthrown die is given to the boxman for scrutiny to prevent strange (or "crooked") dice from being introduced into the game. The remaining dice are offered to the shooter to select a replacement—unless he requests "Same dice please," in which case the game is held up until the misthrown die is retrieved. No bets are won or lost, and players are free to change their wagers. If a die is cocked, or not lying flat, the stickman calls it the way the die would have come to rest, and the roll counts.

Never let your hands get in the way of the thrown dice. If the dice hit your hand before coming to rest, it is considered an omen of bad luck. Many veteran craps shooters actually believe this will cause a 7 to be thrown and the shooter and the pass-line bettors to lose. Go along with this superstition—the dealers do. Listen for their admonition: "Watch your hands!" Or "Hands up!"

Table and Layout

An understanding of the layout on the heavy wooden 12-by-3½-foot table is the next order of business (the size varies—some tables are as short as eight feet). The green baize cloth on the surface, a "craps road map" if you like, permits the game to function efficiently. Of course, we dare not do away with it, but if the layout suddenly disappeared, a dice game could still be carried on. But just imagine the dealers trying to remember all the bets some dozen or more players wish to make. The crew is very good, but they are not superhuman. Examine the two outside sections in Exhibit 3. Note that they are symmetrical, so a player can stand anywhere and have access to identical areas. The center section is under control of the stickman with his proposition bets.

I am always surprised by how many visitors to a casino play with real money without understanding the rules and conditions of the games. People who spend days comparison shopping for everything they buy, from groceries to stocks and bonds, blithely toss their money on the table without the slightest idea of where the best and worst bets are. There are over 30 different bets on a craps layout, but fewer than half a dozen offer the odds that make craps the game with the best value in the casino, exceeded only by blackjack when played by very knowledgeable players. Let's make a study of the most frequently made bets, pointing out those that give you the best value, with the idea of getting the most for our money. Refer to Exhibit 3 as you read the following paragraphs.

Come-Out Roll. How do we start? Each player has designated spots on the table where his bets are to be placed, either by him or by the dealer. Once you become familiar with the layout, it's a simple matter to locate and keep track of your bets. The stickman now announces, "The dice are coming out," and one of the players becomes the shooter. Players become eligible to shoot as the dice travel around the table in a clockwise direction, and when a new shooter takes the dice, all players make their bets. The initial throw is called the *come-out roll*, and it establishes the *point*, upon which all other bets are placed. Most gamblers bet on the pass line with the shooter to *make his point*, or throw his winning number before he throws a seven. In craps jargon, this is called *do-side* or *right-side* betting. *Don't-side* betting, on the Don't Pass Bar 12 line, is also referred to by many craps players as *wrong-side* betting.

Pass Line. To shoot, you must make at least a minimum bet on the pass or don't-pass line. Both are shown on the layout in Exhibit 3. So when the dice are pushed in front of you, select two after placing a wager on the pass line, and throw the dice toward the far

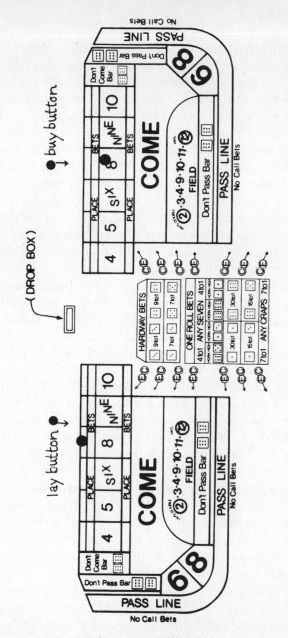

EXHIBIT 3: *Craps Table Layout.*

end of the table. When they come to rest, the numbers appearing skyward are added together and the total is called out by the stickman. The result is your point and it affects your wagers as well as those of all the other players, since some bets can be won or lost on the first roll. If the spots on the dice add up to 7 or 11 on the first throw, called a *natural*, the shooter and the do-bettors win; the don't-bettors lose. This is called a *pass* and the shooter makes a new bet and continues. Should the initial throw total 2, 3, or 12 (called *craps*), the shooter and do-bettors lose; don't-bettors win (except for the *bar 12*—two sixes on the dice—which is a *push*). The shooter does not relinquish the dice, but makes another bet and comes out with a new roll. When the total of the come-out roll is 4, 5, 6, 8, 9, or 10, this number becomes the shooter's point and the number must be repeated before throwing a 7.

After a point is established, a roll of 7 is a loser, rather than the winner it was on the starting or come-out roll. All numbers other than the point or 7 thrown in the meanwhile (including 2, 3, 12, or craps), and 11 (a natural) are waiting numbers and do not alter the pass-line wager in any way. Waiting numbers can be used for other betting situations, which will be discussed later.

When the shooter establishes a point, the dealer places a marker called a *puck* on the appropriate number near the top of the layout. Since there are more ways to make a 7 than any other point, the casino now has the advantage and a pass-line bet can't be removed, although a don't-pass bet can. A don't-bettor would be foolish to cancel his bet, however, as the odds now favor him. Never make a pass-line bet after the come-out roll, since you have lost the opportunity of winning with a natural 7 or 11 on the opening roll. For a similar reason, the house will not permit a don't-pass bet to be made after the initial roll. You can always tell when the shooter is coming out, as the puck will be resting on the Don't Come line with the dark "off" side face up instead of on a number.

After the come-out roll, the shooter continues to throw the dice until a decision is reached, regardless of how many rolls he makes. Should the shooter roll his point, he and the do-bettors win, and the dealer places an equal amount of chips next to his bet. Always remember to pick up your winnings — if they remain on the table, the dealer may assume you are letting it all ride on the next bet.

After making a point, the shooter makes a new bet and repeats the come-out roll procedure. After the point is established, if a 7 should be rolled, the dealer whisks up the losing bets with great speed and without a thank you. The dice now pass to the player on the left of the former shooter, and it becomes her turn to shoot.

The pass line is the most popular area on the layout, and it's where some 80–90% of all players, mostly due to habit and tradition, make their wagers. The percentage for the house, only 1.41%, makes the pass line one of the best bets in the entire casino.

Don't Pass Bar 12. Betting the don't-pass line, often called the *back line*, is just the opposite of betting the pass line, and is preferred by many veteran gamblers. The bet is made on the section of the layout marked Don't Pass Bar 12, and you are betting against the shooter, which could be yourself. Now the appearance of a natural 7 or 11 on the come-out toss will cause you to lose immediately. But when the cubes dance and come to rest exhibiting a 2 or 3 on top, you will experience the thrill of a win, which pays even money. However, craps 12 is a standoff. Neither the casino nor the don't-bettor wins, and the gambler is free to remove his don't-pass wager if he chooses. It is this remarkable piece of arithmetic which permits the casino to bank all bets whether one wagers with or against the dice.

The house, as you recall, enjoys a positive expectation of 1.41 percent on the pass line, and through the expediency of barring the 12 on the don't-pass line, the casino realizes an advantage of 1.40 percent. Thus, the casino holds a slight advantage on both lines.

If you bet the don't-pass line, when the shooter rolls a point and then misses out, you win. If he makes his point, you lose. We have learned that most people wager on the pass line. Perhaps only 10 percent are wrong-bettors, possibly because of the pessimistic connotation. It's unnatural for most gamblers not to be able to call with the other bettors for a natural on the come-out roll and for a steady stream of passes. Nevertheless, don't-pass is not an erroneous or poor bet; on the contrary, it is one of the best bets in the casino.

Come Bets. The *come bet*, made only after a point is established, is exactly the same as a pass-line bet except you can bet the come any time you want—not just on a come-out roll. The very next roll of the dice establishes this new bet. If the shooter throws a 4, 5, 6, 8, 9, or 10, the stickman moves your bet to a specific spot in the appropriate number box on the layout, which indicates that it's your bet.

As with a pass-line bet, a come bet cannot be taken down. Of course, if the roll had been 2, 3, or 12, your come bet would have been a loser. An 11 would have won. A next roll of 7 would have been a winner, but the pass-line bet would lose. With a come bet in the number box, you are pulling for the shooter to repeat this number before a 7. If he does, you win even money; if he sevens out, you lose. When you win, the stickman places your winnings plus your original bet in front of you on the come line. Be sure to pick it up before the next roll of the dice or you will have a new come bet for the total amount.

Everyone at the table, including a new arrival or the shooter, can make a come bet on all subsequent tosses of the dice after the come-out roll. It's obvious that betting the come line before every roll of the dice can result in a very exciting and profitable situation if the dice stay away from 7. Of course, the 7 becomes a real threat after a number of come bets have been made, since it will wipe out the pass line as well as all the come bets. Even after the pass-line number is made, you are not looking for a natural 7 on a come-out roll, as it wipes out all the come bets in the number boxes, which we have learned can't be taken down. The dreaded 7 loses most of your bets, but it represents a winner on a final bet on the come line. Sometimes, players leave the table, forgetting this last winner. The house advantage on come bets is 1.41 percent, exactly the same as the pass-line bet.

Place Bets. *Place bets* are by far the most popular number bets and resemble come bets in that you are betting on a particular number to be thrown before the 7. The difference is that your money goes right to the number instead of to the come line. Thus, if you put a bet on the table and announce to the dealer, "Place the 5," your chips are put on your designated spot in the place-5 box on the layout. If a 5 is thrown before 7, you win and are paid off at 7-to-5 odds. The dealer will place your winnings in front of you and ask, "Same bet?" You can say, "Yes," and let the bet stay up on the placed number; "Take it down," and your bet will be returned; or "Press it," and enough of your winnings will be taken to double your bet.

Your odds on placing the 5 are not very good—the house advantage is 4 percent. If you place the 9, the house advantage is the same 4 percent. Placing the numbers 4 and 10 are even worse, yielding the casino 6.67 percent. A place bet on the 6 or 8 is a completely different matter; the casino advantage of 1.52 percent is just slightly more than the 1.41 percent for come bets.

Aggressive come bettors, eager for action, sometimes place the 6 and 8 right after the come-out roll, replacing the wager with a come bet if the number comes up. You must make place bets in increments of $6 to take full advantage of the odds when you place the 6 or 8. If you place the 4, 5, 9, or 10, you must bet in increments of $5 at the $5 minimum tables. If you bet less than $5, you will be paid even money. If you bet more, you will be paid the odds on the next lower amount.

Many craps players believe that place betting gives them a better deal, and the house less of an advantage, than come betting. This is not true. Come betting gives the house a small advantage of 1.41 percent, as compared to place-betting advantages ranging from 1.52 percent to 6.67 percent. Why the large difference? Because when you make a come bet, you have a chance for an immediate winner when a natural 7 or 11 is thrown. It's true that you also lose immediately when craps 2, 3, or 12 is rolled, but this occurs only half as often.

Some players like to have all the numbers working for them immediately. "$32 across the board" means place $5 on each of the numbers 4, 5, 9, and 10, and $6 each on the 6 and 8. The 4 and 10 pay off at 9 to 5; the 5 and 9 pay off at 7 to 5; and the 6 and 8 pay off at 7 to 6. Thus, for every number the shooter rolls, the place bettor has a winner. The come bettor must wait for a number to be rolled twice before he can win — once to establish his point and the second time to win.

Place betting in this manner can be very dangerous to your bankroll. In addition to giving the casino a much higher advantage, five numbers must be rolled before you recoup your investment. A 7 thrown early in the series will wipe out your $32 bet with little, if any, return. I have seen many players walk up to a table and say, "$32 across the board," only to have a 7 on the very next roll wipe out their entire bet. In come betting, your entire investment is not risked all at once. Also, a seven out early in the series is a winner for you; 7 is a winner for the last come bet.

Field Bets. A *field bet*, positioned by the player, is a one-roll bet. Unlike a pass-line bet, which occurs over a series of rolls, your field bet is won or lost on the next roll of the dice. This wager can be made at any time, and to the beginning craps player, the field bet appears to be a really good bet. After all, you've covered 7 of the 11 numbers: 3, 4, 9, 10, and 11 pay even money, and the 2 and 12 pay double. You lose only if the 5, 6, 7, or 8 comes up. However, if you examine the number of combinations in which each number can be rolled, it turns out you would lose 20 units and win 18 for every 38 units wagered. This equates to a casino advantage of over 5 percent. The field bet is definitely not a good bet to make. You are much better off sticking to the pass and come line, where the house advantage is only 1.41 percent.

Proposition Bets. "Five dollars on any craps. Okay, who wants the eleven? Ten on the hard four." The stickman at the craps table is like a circus barker, standing in the center of the table and controlling the flow of the game. His primary job is to entice the players into making *proposition bets*. I call them sucker bets because the odds against you are extremely high: the casino edge ranges from 9.09 to 16.67 percent. Because of the extremely high odds against you, I am placing these bets outside the scope of this book and, with one exception, I do not recommend any of them.

The only time you should consider a proposition bet is if you are winning big money and in the middle of a hot streak. Then, betting "Any Craps" is a good insurance bet against your big pass-line bet. For example, suppose you've been winning on a hot roll and have built your pass-line bet up to $25. A 2, 3, or 12 would wipe this out and perhaps discourage you from betting another $25 on the next come-out roll. However, an insurance bet of $3 or $4 on Any Craps would recoup enough to justify another $25 bet. Any Craps pays 7 to 1, so your $3 bet would return $21; your $4 bet would return $28. Use this win, adding $4 to the $21 or taking $3 from the $28, to make your next pass-line bet. You have no need to make another Any Craps wager, as your last one remains on that bet for the next come-out roll.

Free Odds. The first and foremost thing to remember is that this bet is paid at the correct odds; therefore, you have an even chance of winning. Thus, if the point number is 4 and the odds are taken, say, for $5, the house will pay $10 for winning this 2-to-1 wager. Remember, the house enjoys an edge on every play at the table except this one. You can take advantage of the free-odds bet only if you have already made a wager on the pass line, don't pass, come, or don't come.

"Taking the odds" is the correct phrasing when a wager is made on the pass or come line. This bet is also known as a *right bet*, and the player is, of course, a *right-bettor*. When a point is established— 4, 5, 6, 8, 9, or 10—the bet is backed up by placing the odds wager directly behind the pass-line bet. Taking single odds on pass and come bets reduces the casino advantage from 1.41 percent to 0.85 percent.

It is important to memorize the free odds so you can be paid off at the maximum rate. Backup bets on 5 and 9 should be made in increments of $2 so the bet can be paid off at the rate of 3 to 2. The 6 and 8 should be backed up in increments of $5 so the bet can be paid off at 6 to 5. The numbers of 4 and 10 never become a problem, as the payoff rate is 2 to 1. In most casinos, your backup bet may not exceed twice the initial bet. For instance, if your pass-line bet is $4, your backup bet would be either $4 or $8 if the come-out number is 5 or 9. With a come-out number of 6 or 8, the backup bet to receive a 6-to-5 payoff would be $5 or $10.

The free-odds bet is central to all my advice on money management. Many craps authors advise always taking maximum odds. This is bad advice; you may be risking too much of your bankroll. In Chapter 11, I will show you that your advantage with a controlled throw doesn't increase that much on taking odds of greater than 3 to 1. The same holds if you're playing into the house advantage without a controlled throw; don't take more than three times your pass-line bet even if the casino offers 5 times odds or greater (some casinos will permit you to take as much as 10 times odds).

The other point I want to make on free odds right now is never, never lay the odds if you are playing the don't side. When the point is established, you have the advantage when playing the don't side. Why give back part of it by laying the odds? There is also too much risk involved because you are always betting more than you are getting back.

ADVICE FOR RECREATIONAL PLAYERS

The next five chapters are devoted to laying the foundation for and then describing a rhythm roll method for achieving a player advantage at casino craps. Even if you're an occasional gambler or a recreational player, I believe you will benefit greatly by reading each one of them. However, if your interests are just in getting some good approaches to betting and improving your table play, you could skip over to Chapters 13 and 14.

Ten

STATE-OF-THE-ART ADVANTAGE CRAPS SYSTEMS

THE CONTROLLED THROW

How would you like to walk up to a craps table knowing that you had an excellent chance of creating a hot table, that when your turn came to pick up the dice, you could throw number after number without the seven showing?

How would it feel to make come bets and place bets with the confidence of knowing that you were going to collect winnings, sometimes substantial winnings, before sevening out?

If you've ever been at a hot table, you know the excitement. Chips stacking up on all the numbers. Players yelling and even screaming. Dealers pushing huge stacks of chips to players on the winning points. Numbers coming up roll after roll, with many players collecting on every roll. Pit bosses hovering over the table with nervous looks.

If you're a craps player, you've been there. It's by far the most exciting part of gambling for any of the casino games.

This is what a controlled throw or rhythm roll is all about—to put you in a position to create that hot table and to fill that rack of chips in front of you. Not every time, mind you. But often enough to create some fantastic profit possibilities.

Is this possible, you ask—to alter the random outcome of the dice? To actually create your own advantage over the casinos? Everything ever written about the game states otherwise. "A game of independent trials" is what the gambling experts call it, with each throw being totally random and independent of every other throw.

Well then, how about the casinos? Surely they know whether it's possible to control the dice, don't they? Some do and some don't. Try to set the dice in some casino locations and dealers admonish you not to. Step up to a table in other locations and you can set the dice any way you want (as long as you don't hold up the game). But knowledgeable dealers who have been around craps tables for a few years will tell you they've seen rhythm rollers.

What the Experts Say

Few gambling experts will admit that a controlled throw is possible and can lead to a player advantage. Peter Griffin (the great blackjack guru, now deceased) states on page 1 of his book *Extra Stuff* (Huntington Press, 1991) that it is possible to achieve an advantage by executing a controlled throw. He tells the story of how "Sal" used a controlled throw to achieve a 67 percent advantage! What Sal did was slide one die down the table right along the bottom so it came to rest on the six. An accomplice then laid a big bet on the field. Since field numbers include the 9 (6–3), 10 (6–4), 11 (6–5) and 12 (6–6), Sal had four chances out of six to win this bet, thus a 67 percent advantage.

Steve Forte, one of the most successful blackjack players ever, wrote a book called *Read the Dealer* (RGE, 1986) and because of it most casinos today don't let dealers peek at their hole cards until after all players' hands have been played. Steve, now a consultant to the gaming industry, demonstrated a controlled throw for a group of students at the William F. Harrah Institute of Casino Entertainment. He rolled three double sixes in succession—about 46,000-to-1 shot!

These two examples—Sal and Steve Forte—of sliding one die along the tabletop so it comes to rest at the end of the throw exactly where it started in the beginning (the 6), are now outlawed by the casinos. The dice must be thrown above the tabletop. The next time you shoot craps, notice the "string" in the middle of the table. This is to stop a sliding die.

Our approach to a controlled throw as defined in Chapter 12 is perfectly legal. We will not slide the dice down the table as Sal and Steve did. We will throw them in a nice high arc above the tabletop so they land one or two inches from the back wall, and then roll up and tap it gently (which most casinos require) before coming to rest.

If you're a craps player, you've probably seen at least one or two shooters with controlled throws or rhythm rolls. But you didn't recognize a possible advantage, so you probably ignored them. I guarantee that in reading this book, you will take a much closer look at these craps shooters—their set, their throw, and their result—even if you don't develop a controlled throw of your own.

The state of the art of legal controlled throws, with an arc above the tabletop but not too high (certainly not higher than the stickman's head), is essentially described in this book. To understand and appreciate my recommendations in this book for developing a controlled throw and achieving an advantage, you really have to know where I'm coming from in my own developmental efforts, because the current state of the art resulted from my pioneering work in this arena.

How the Controlled Throw Was Developed

Back in the early 1980s, when I was the gambling columnist for the *Philadelphia Inquirer*, I was besieged with requests from my readers to teach a class on craps and roulette (I had been teaching blackjack classes for quite some time—how to win at card counting).

So I organized a class and taught a group of serious gamblers the rudiments of craps and roulette and a few simple betting tactics so they could take advantage of winning streaks and avoid giving all their money away too quickly.

An elderly gentleman in the class didn't say much until the second session. I noticed his rapt attention and knew he had something on his mind. Finally, he broke his silence, picked up the dice, and said: "I can show you guys how to beat this game."

Immediately, all eyes were on him, including my own. What he did was set the dice before throwing them, with his number on top and the losing 7 relegated to the inside and outside of the dice. He then proceeded to call out which numbers he would throw and, usually, within two or three rolls, up would pop that number.

He was not only setting the dice but also using what we now call a *controlled throw* or *rhythm roll*. His objective was to alter the random outcome of the dice, and he was accomplishing this objective by avoiding the losing 7. His technique involved "sliding" the dice down the felt, which was permissible in the games he banked and was allowed in the casinos at that time.

"How many years did it take you to develop this skill?" I asked. "I perfected this while serving in the Army back in World War II," he said. "We used to call it the old 'Army blanket roll.' Won a nice little stake and used it to start my own business after the war."

My mind snapped shut like a trapdoor. I immediately assumed that it would take hundreds of hours of practice to perfect this technique for casino play, which I didn't have the patience to invest. I was so wrapped up in blackjack card counting and shuffle tracking at the time that I didn't have the foresight to realize what he was showing me.

In the mid-1980s, another opportunity to observe the controlled throw presented itself. A friend of mine demonstrated his controlled throw in the casino. He set the dice in his own way, stood at the end of the table, and threw them in a high arc toward the far end. His objective was to get enough height to minimize their forward movement after landing at the far end—just enough to tap the end of the table, as the casinos require, and avoid the losing 7. His only problem was he threw the dice too high, above the stickman's head, and the casino wouldn't allow the throw.

His demonstration was successful and we won a little money. Near the end, however, the stickman batted the dice out of the air with his stick, picked them up, and said, "That's enough of that."

But this second glimpse into the winning arena came at a time when I was still too preoccupied with blackjack to recognize the possibilities. And it wasn't for another five years, in the early 1990s, that I began to study these methods for altering the natural odds of craps and gaining an edge over the house.

Although I have been shooting craps ever since my first trip to the casino in 1956, I played only to unwind after a tough session at the blackjack tables. It was, and still is, my favorite game, but purely for fun.

Then began one of the most fantastic winning streaks of my gambling career. There were periods when I won 15 to 20 craps sessions in a row—some with small wins and some with big. I took this streak in stride in the beginning, thinking that things were evening up, that I was due because of prior losses. But the streak continued with intermittent stoppages on short-term losing streaks. Not wanting to give back my winnings, I would just cease play for a few weeks, a month or even a few months during this four-year period.

In early 1996 when another incredible streak began, I started to really analyze my play. I realized that I was shooting differently—that subconsciously, I had developed a controlled throw, not setting the dice, but throwing them the same way every time, or at least trying to—an easy muscle-memory rhythm roll.

I was also watching the other shooters with a more observant eye, attempting to discern those shooters that could hold the dice for a while. I noticed that, at some tables and during some sessions, I couldn't do anything right, while in others I couldn't do anything wrong.

Everything came together on a trip to Turning Stone casino in July 1996. I watched a shooter hold the dice for 25 minutes with a controlled throw. I didn't just watch, I participated in the excitement—the table cleaned up. Then I got "in the zone" and held the dice for 20 minutes.

I shared my findings with my associate, Eric Nielsen. The next day I invited him to watch me play. We waited a few minutes for me to get the dice—and then I quickly sevened out.

But I wasn't discouraged, because I felt good. The next time I got the dice, I held them for 20 minutes. Eric was amazed. The table was cold when I got there, with player after player walking away muttering to themselves.

My second time with the dice turned it from cold to hot, and the shouting began. When I left the game, you couldn't get near the table, it was so packed with players all wanting to get a piece of the action.

On my way home to Carson City from that trip, I stopped at the Reno Hilton. I got my spot at a table with a few players, but not much was going on. A player to my right, on the end of the table to the right of the stickman, got the dice. Then I saw the most beautiful exhibition of a controlled throw I've ever seen, including my own. He held the dice for 25 minutes and everybody was cleaning up, including the dealers, whom he was toking generously.

You could see the casino's chips evaporating with each successive throw, including the 20-chip stacks of blacks. Three pit bosses were hovering behind the boxman watching the payoffs. It took 20 to 30 seconds between each throw to pay everyone off for the last number thrown.

When he sevened out, he got a 20-second round of applause, with the dealers applauding too. It took five minutes to color everyone up. Orange chips ($1,000) were disappearing quickly on the color-up.

This shooter was in a groove, a zone. It's like when you see a shooter get hot in a basketball game, or a baseball player go on a hitting streak, or a roulette dealer get into a groove when spinning the wheel.

Over the next year, I worked with my associates and a number of network members to perfect the controlled throw. Before I get to the details, let me answer two common questions that occur for most craps players when they consider the possibility of a controlled throw:

1. *Do I have to know how to play the game to learn and use a controlled throw?* No. You don't have to know a thing about

the game to use the method. You'll learn all you need to in this book—it shouldn't take more than 15 minutes to learn what craps is all about.

2. *Does it require much skill and coordination to develop a rhythm roll?* Is it difficult? It depends. Most gamblers require many hours of practice; some don't. But I've personally taught players and seen them walk into a casino a couple of hours later, execute the controlled throw, and win.

The answer to this question is where the controversy about controlled throws begins. The controversy goes something like this: How can you get any control when you release the dice in a medium-arced throw, peaking a couple of feet above the tabletop, with the dice landing and bumping up against the front wall into those diamond-shaped bumpers and then finally coming to rest?

My answer to the skeptics is that it takes only 1 controlled throw out of 43, with the other 42 random, to alter the random outcome of the game to an even game for the 6 and 8 place bets. We've done the computations. They are beyond the scope of this book, but if you would like this information, contact me using the coupon at the back of this book and I'll send you a complimentary copy. I urge you to keep an open mind! Employing a controlled throw and setting the dice will alter the random outcome of the game and lead to your advantage in casino craps.

You will notice that I have been using the two terms *controlled throw* and *rhythm roll* interchangeably to this point in the book. They mean the same thing.

Before you read the description of the advantage method, it is necessary for you to understand how and why an advantage can be achieved. In Chapter 11, we define and calculate the player advantage. I think you'll find these calculations interesting and fairly easy to understand. However, those readers not interested in the arithmetic may wish to turn right to Chapter 12.

Eleven

CALCULATING THE PLAYER ADVANTAGE FOR CRAPS

In this chapter and the next, you will learn how to achieve an advantage at casino craps by altering the natural outcome of two die tossed by a shooter. *Altering the natural outcome* are the key words here. The natural outcome is random, and this is what 99 percent of gamblers and gambling writers have believed that craps is all about since craps was invented.

You can alter the natural outcome in one of two ways: (1) by setting the dice with certain combinations of numbers on top, and (2) by executing a rhythm roll. In this book, you will learn how to do both and achieve an advantage at casino craps.

AVOIDING THE LOSING 7

Achieving an advantage is all about avoiding the losing 7, and the rhythm roll is executed to avoid the losing 7. The longer you hold the dice without throwing the losing 7, the higher your advantage and the more money you can make. It's as simple as that. On the first throw of a new cycle (called the "come-out" in craps jargon, that is, coming out for a new number), the 7 and 11 are winners while the 2, 3, and 12 are losers. Any other number is your *point*—4, 5, 6, 8, 9, and 10.

Once your point is established, the 7 becomes the losing number and your objective is to avoid it at all costs, because as long as you avoid the 7 and keep throwing "numbers" (craps jargon for 4, 5, 6, 8, 9, and 10), you keep on winning (2, 3, 11, and 12 are neutral numbers, not losers, and 11 is not a winning throw after the come-out roll and the point is established).

Again, this is what a rhythm roll is all about—avoiding the losing 7.

The Seven-to-Rolls Ratio

Let's take a closer look at this losing number, since it's what achieving an advantage is all about. Examine Figure 4, which shows the frequency distribution of all possible outcomes of two dice. This table shows how many times each number will be rolled compared to every other number. It is based on a standard 36-roll sample size.

Notice that out of 36 combinations for throwing the two dice, six of them are 7s. Therefore, a 7 will be rolled about once every six rolls of the dice (36 divided by 6). So 6 times out of 36 is random, and this ratio of 1 in 6 is what yields the casino advantage at casino craps.

The simple purpose of the rhythm roll is to increase the random number of one 7 every six rolls to a higher number—the higher the better. We introduce the term *seven-to-rolls ratio* (SRR) to define the number of times the dice are rolled before a 7 shows during the point cycle—that is, when the shooter has established and is rolling for a point number (4, 5, 6, 8, 9, 10). An SRR of 6 is random. Note that a skilled rhythm roller could set and aim for the 7 on the come-out roll where the 7 wins, so the come-out does not factor into our calculation of the seven-to-rolls ratio.

We have calculated that an SRR of 6.14 for the 6 and 8 place bets (betting that a 6 or 8 will be rolled before the 7) is break-even. How difficult is it to achieve this 6.14? Here's another way of looking at it: rolling seven 7s every 42 rolls equates to an SRR of 6 (42

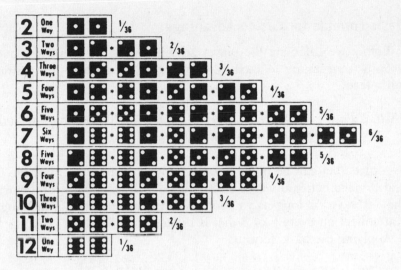

FIGURE 4: *Distribution of All Possible Dice Outcomes*

divided by 7) or random. But seven 7s every 43 rolls equates to an SRR of 6.14 (43 divided by 7), or break-even. Just one non-random or rhythm roll every 43 tosses of the dice is all it takes to eliminate the casino advantage! This breakthrough calculation is beyond the scope of this book. If you would like a complimentary copy, contact me using the coupon at the back of the book. But it is possible to do a lot better than only one rhythm roll every 43 throws, as I'll show you later in this chapter.

To give you an understanding of how and why you can achieve an advantage over the casino, follow along with me through two calculations: (1) calculation of casino advantage for the 6 and 8 place bets, and (2) calculation of a rhythm roller's advantage for 6 and 8 place bets. Sharpshooter, my associate and craps instructor, performed these breakthrough calculations.

Basic Formula for Casino Advantage:

Before we calculate the player advantage for the 6 and 8 place bets, it is necessary to establish a point of departure—the casino advantage.

[Actual Payoff − Correct Payoff] × Probability of Outcome × 100 percent = percent Casino Advantage

A place bet can be made on any number at any time. For the 6 and 8 place bet, you wager $6 to win $7 that the 6 will roll before the 7 shows. As long as you roll the dice without the 7 showing, you collect on every 6 or 8 that is rolled.

Applying the basic formula:

[7/6 − 6/5] × 5/11 × 100 percent = 1.515 percent Casino Advantage

Explanation. 7 to 6 is what the casino pays, but the actual odds of a 6 or 8 occurring before a 7 are 6 to 5. The probability of outcome, that is, a 6 rolling before a 7, is 5/11 because the 6 has 5 chances of hitting out of 36 rolls, while the 7 has 6 chances in 36 of being rolled. Simple probability theory for just these two events— 5 chances for the 6 or 8, and 6 chances for the 7, or a total of 11 chances—says that the probability of outcome of the 6 or 8 is 5 divided by 11, or 5/11.

Calculating the Player Advantage for 6 and 8 Place Bets

We have stated earlier that a player break-even point is achieved when the shooter accomplishes a seven-to-rolls ratio (SRR) of 6.14. Therefore, a player advantage is achieved by surpassing 6.14.

I have found through my own experience and teaching others that a skilled rhythm roller can accomplish an SRR of 8. So an SRR of 8 is used as the assumption for computing the player advantage for the 6 and 8 place bets.

But in assuming the shooter has achieved a SRR of 1:8 (that is,

1:6 S.R.R. FREQUENCY DISTRIBUTION
(6 sevens in 36 trials, random)

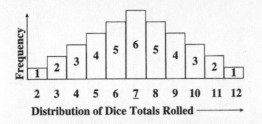

FIGURE 5: *Bar Chart of Frequency Distribution of All Possible Dice Outcomes*

one 7 every eight rolls), I must change the random-outcome distribution shown in Figure 4, which is shown as a bar chart in Figure 5, to reflect a SRR of 1:8. Therefore, I must alter the random-outcome distribution shown in Figures 4 and 5 and use a *weighted distribution*. This is shown in Figure 6, which I will now discuss.

Figure 5 is easily understood by considering a standard of 36 rolls of the dice: 7 occurs six times, 6 and 8 occur five times, and so on. Adding up the frequency of occurrence, you get 36.

But now we change this frequency distribution to factor in our advantage—of a 7 occurring only once every eight rolls instead of once every six rolls. To make the calculations easy to understand, we'll use a sample size of 48 rolls instead of 36. I construct a weighted outcome distribution of 48 rolls, including six 7s (48 rolls divided by six 7s equals 8, or one 7 every eight rolls; SRR = 8).

To figure the distribution of the other outcomes (2s, 3s, 4s, 5s, 6s, 8s, 9s, 10s, 11s, 12s) in this new 48-roll frequency distribution chart, I need a weighted average. Factoring the 7 out of our calculation, there are 42 outcomes left out of 48. In a random distribution, there are 30 outcomes left after the six 7s are factored out. So I divided 42 by 30 to get our weighted average of 1.4 for the other outcomes.

I multiply 1.4 by each outcome of the random distribution to get the new weighted average for each outcome. For example, we mul-

1:8 S.R.R. FREQUENCY DISTRIBUTION
(6 sevens in 48 trials)

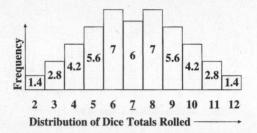

Distribution of Dice Totals Rolled ──────➤

FIGURE 6: *Altered Frequency Distribution for 6 and 8 Place Bets with SRR = 8*

tiply the random outcome for 6 and 8, which is 5 times every 36 rolls as follows: 5 times 1.4 equals 7; therefore, 6 and 8 occur seven times in our new frequency distribution. (See Figure 6.)

From this new distribution, we can now compute the advantage based on an SRR of 1:8 instead of 1:6. I use the same formula I used before to compute the casino advantage, except this time I derive the player advantage. That formula is:

[Actual Payoff − Correct Payoff] × Probability of Outcome × 100 percent = percent Player Advantage

The actual payoff is still 7 to 6. The correct payoff, or odds of occurrence, for our new distribution is now 6 to 7 instead of 6 to 5. Since we, the player, have an edge, the "correct" payoff (if the casino were to factor in our advantage), is less than even money— $6 for each $7 bet. Thus, the probability of outcome changes from 5/11 to 7/13.

So our calculation looks like this:

[7/6 − 6/7] × 7/13 × 100 percent = 16.67 percent Player Advantage.

The player now has an advantage of 16.7 percent over the casino (assuming, of course, that he or she can develop the skill to achieve a SRR of 1:8).

We started this discussion by stating that out of 43 rolls, 42 could be random, but if that 43rd roll is controlled to alter the natural outcome of the dice and avoid the losing 7, the house advantage is eliminated! It takes very little skill to create a positive advantage for the player! In our calculation, we have assumed that the player is rolling one 7 every eight rolls of the dice, for an SRR of 8. But you don't have to accomplish an SRR of 8 to gain an advantage — anything over 6.14 will do.

For the other place bets, we have calculated that the break-even point for the 5 and 9 place bets (which pay $7 for each $5 wagered) is one 7 every 6.36 rolls. For the 4 and 10 place bets (which pay $9 for each $5 wagered), the break-even point is one 7 every 6.56 rolls.

These break-even points were used to calculate the player advantages shown in Exhibit 4. Notice how the player advantage varies with the SRR for each place bet: 6 and 8, 5 and 9, and 4 and 10.

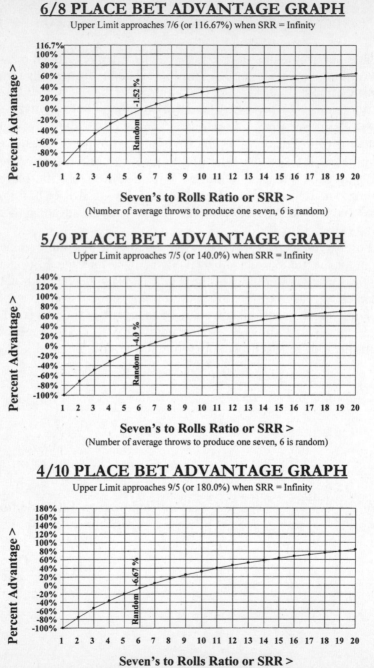

6/8 PLACE BET ADVANTAGE GRAPH

Upper Limit approaches 7/6 (or 116.67%) when SRR = Infinity

Percent Advantage >

Random -1.52 %

Seven's to Rolls Ratio or SRR >

(Number of average throws to produce one seven, 6 is random)

5/9 PLACE BET ADVANTAGE GRAPH

Upper Limit approaches 7/5 (or 140.0%) when SRR = Infinity

Percent Advantage >

Random -4.0 %

Seven's to Rolls Ratio or SRR >

(Number of average throws to produce one seven, 6 is random)

4/10 PLACE BET ADVANTAGE GRAPH

Upper Limit approaches 9/5 (or 180.0%) when SRR = Infinity

Percent Advantage >

Random -6.67 %

Seven's to Rolls Ratio or SRR >

(Number of average throws to produce one seven, 6 is random)

EXHIBIT 4: *Graphs of Player Advantages for All Place Bets with Varying SRRs*

Using the same approach as before for the 6 and 8 place bets, we have also calculated the player advantages for pass-line bets with alternative-odds bets. Table 2 is a summary of the player advantages for the pass line calculated for an SRR of 8. The advantages are expressed as percentages rounded to the nearest tenth. Here is a simple explanation of a 10 percent player advantage: Out of every 100 bets, the advantage player will win 55 and lose 45 (55 − 45 = 10 percent).

Pass line with no odds: 9.5 percent

Pass line with single odds: 13.9 percent

Pass line with double odds: 15.8 percent

Pass line with triple odds: 16.8 percent

Pass line with 5 times odds: 17.9 percent

Pass line with 10 times odds: 19 percent

Pass line with 100 times odds: 20.3 percent

Pass line with 1000 times odds: 20.45 percent

Pass line with infinite odds: 20.47 percent

TABLE 2: *Player Advantages for the Pass Line with Varying-Odds Bets with SRR = 8*

As you can see by the numbers in Table 2, very little additional advantage is derived on odds bets greater than triple. But let's get to the bottom line. Enough of this technical stuff. But wasn't it interesting? And it should give you the confidence to proceed with enthusiasm! Let's proceed to Chapter 12 for a description on how to execute a rhythm roll.

Twelve

THE RHYTHM ROLL FOR ADVANTAGE CRAPS

The basic theory of the rhythm roll is that if you throw the dice the same way every time, in the same trajectory with the same velocity, and if they land in the same spot at the end of the table a couple of inches from the back wall, the outcome will be the same.

And if the dice are set in such a way that the 7 is not on one of the four faces, then, theoretically, a 7 will not occur. In a perfect world, then, you can avoid the 7 forever, take your fortune off the table, cash out, and retire.

But in the real world, theory does not, of course, hold on every roll. In fact, it is difficult to execute a rhythm roll every time. But, in Chapter 11, we discussed that only one rhythm roll in every 43 tosses is all that's needed to break even with the casino. And, by combining a rhythm roll with setting the dice, you can alter the natural outcome a high percentage of the time. So it's worth the effort to learn how to do it.

What's the best way? There is no simple answer to this question, because everyone is different. What may work for me may not work for you. You have to experiment to find the best way for you.

Here are a few factors to consider when developing your rhythm roll:

- Throwing overhand (palm up) or underhand (palm down)

- Imparting "spin" or no "spin" as you launch the dice into their trajectory

- Using a high, medium or low trajectory; i.e., how high should you throw the dice?

- The landing—how close to the back wall should you aim?

- Your spot at the table—where should you stand?

I will discuss these factors as a two-step description of the rhythm roll: the set and the delivery.

SETTING THE DICE

Let's start with the set or positioning of the dice. How do you set the dice prior to the throw? What numbers should be on the top, bottom, and sides?

There are 1,152 different combinations of how two die can be positioned. You can witness the many variations by observing craps shooters in the casino who use a set. Some set the dice on the point; others use some standard number that may be their favorite lucky number.

I'll never forget one evening in the old Playboy Club in Atlantic City, when I was standing next to a shooter setting the dice on the two ones. He would position the dice so that the ones were straight up and then chant "the eyes, the eyes" prior to the throw. (In craps jargon, ones are known as "snake eyes" or "the eyes.") So you'll see all kinds of sets at the table. What amazes me is the care many shooters use to set the dice, then pick them up and throw them haphazardly down the table with no rhythm roll whatsoever.

The 6-T Set. The set I will teach you here is very effective and, with practice, will achieve a player advantage. It's called the 6-T Set

FIGURE 7A: *The 6-T Set—Example 1*   FIGURE 7B: *The 6-T Set—Example 2*

because the two sixes are arranged in a T formation, as shown in Figures 7a and 7b.

It's as simple as that. Arrange the two dice with the sixes on top as shown, without regard to what's on the two sides or the bottom, and you're ready to pick them up and throw.

Get out a pair of die, set a 6-T, and take a look at the sides and bottom. You won't see any 7s! When you practice this set at home, keep one thing in mind: You must execute the set with one hand only while the dice are resting on the table. This is a casino rule to prevent unscrupulous players from slipping loaded dice into the game. To avoid undue attention, practice this set until you can execute it in two seconds or less.

Quick Set. If you don't want to fool with the dice, use what I call the Quick Set. Its purpose is to ensure no 7s are showing on the four faces of the dice. If no 7s are showing, then there is less chance that a 7 will occur when the dice land and come to a halt at the end of their trajectory.

The way to execute the Quick Set is to examine the dice in the middle of the table before the stickman pushes them back to you for your next throw. Look at the closest side visible to you. If there's a 7 showing on this side, there will also be one on the other side. To get rid of the 7 on both sides, just flick one die a quarter turn either toward you or away from you. This will take both 7s off the two sides.

Experienced craps shooters know that the stickman will never return the dice to the shooter with a 7 on top. This is considered not only bad luck but extremely rude, and if the dice should happen to tumble onto a 7 as they're returned to you, the stickman will usually apologize and reset them to a non-7.

Seven on Front · Right Die Rotated Forward

FIGURE 7C: *The Quick Set with 7 on the Front, Then with Right Die Rotated Forward*

Seven on Front · Left Die Rotated Forward

FIGURE 7D: *The Quick Set with 7 on the Front, Then with Left Die Rotated Forward*

But he will not set them so a 7 doesn't show on the side. You have to do this. The Quick Set is illustrated in Figures 7c and 7d.

THE DELIVERY

So now we're ready to execute the rhythm roll and launch the dice into their trajectory. Consideration should be given to comfort, control, and consistency. Try a few delivery systems and select one that feels right for your anatomy. Attempt it from different spots on the table so you'll find the spot that's most comfortable for you.

After setting, pick up the dice the same way each time. After you pick them up the first few times, turn your wrist so you can observe how you are holding them. Are your fingers situated around the dice the same way each time you pick them up? Is the holding force you apply comfortable and balanced? You want just enough gripping force to keep the dice steady during the release, but not too excessive, which might cause the dice to "squirt" from your hand.

An important part of the delivery is the way you grip the dice.

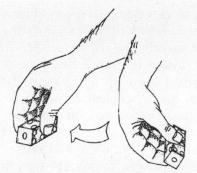

FIGURE 8A: *Underhand Delivery*

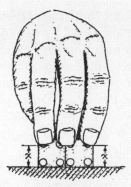

FIGURE 8B: *Three-Fingered Front Grip*

There are several types of grips and throws you can try. Space limitations prevent me from describing and illustrating them all; however, I will show you Sharpshooter's grip which he calls the "three-fingered front." Figure 8a illustrates this grip and also his delivery; notice he uses an underhand throw (palm down) and notice his hand movement which produces a nice smooth delivery.

Figure 8b illustrates this grip from the front. Notice the parallel fingers and the loose "pinky."

Try this one, but you should also experiment with others to find the grip best suited for you. One of the benefits of attending our course is the personalized instruction for critiquing your throw and for assisting you to find that grip and throw which work best for you. Details are in the appendix.

Follow through and throw the dice. Do they initially land in the same general area? Note the position of your hand each time you throw. Is it consistent? Is your arm extended the same way throw after throw?

Deliver the dice with just enough energy to reach the intended target, which should be two or three inches from the back wall.

You can practice your throw at home by throwing on the kitchen table, on the bed, or into an open dresser drawer. When you try this in the casino, go to a low-limit table—$2 or $5 if possible. Try to go at times when the tables are not so crowded so you can quickly get the dice back when you lose your turn with the dice by throwing a 7 (known as *sevening out* in craps jargon).

When you become adept at your rhythm roll, you'll find yourself with a problem to overcome—avoiding the chip stacks at the far end of the table! Other players will raise their bets as you make successive passes and throw lots of numbers. If you hit a stack of chips, your throw obviously loses control and you're at the mercy of the gods of chance. You may not throw a 7, but it's more likely.

I'll never forget the end of one of my longest throws. It began in a very crowded casino in Atlantic City. There were only a few spots open, but I did find my favorite position at one table. I bellied up, quickly got the dice, and held them for 30 minutes, throwing number after number without the 7 showing except on the come-out rolls. The players were yelling and screaming and the chips were stacking up. My racks were filled with green, black, and purple and I was "in a zone"—I felt that I could hold the dice all night.

But, alas it was not to be. On my last throw, one die hit a stack of chips and then bounced, coming to rest right on top of the stack—a six. Immediately, without looking, I knew what the other die would be—a one. The dreaded 7 had finally reared its ugly head. The only happy people were the three pit bosses who were hovering behind the table watching the payoffs to make sure they were correct.

If you wish to consider detailed instruction to develop your rhythm roll—setting the dice and executing the controlled throw—a brief description of the Sharpshooter Craps home study course is contained in the appendix along with instructions for contacting the author.

Thirteen

BETTING TACTICS FOR
ADVANTAGE CRAPS

Three betting alternatives are described, each depending on the level of risk you wish to take:

- **Basic:** The pass-line betting tactic
- **Moderate Risk:** Place betting the 6 and 8
- **Aggressive:** Covering all the numbers

The assumptions for each of these are (1) that you are "grooved in," throwing in the advantage zone with a SRR greater than 6.5; (2) that you are playing with a 100-unit bankroll, and (3) that your basic bet size is one unit. If you're playing at a $5 minimum table, you must have at least $500 in your bankroll. I will use the $5 and $500 assumption in the examples that follow.

BETTING TACTIC 1: THE PASS-LINE BETTING TACTIC

This tactic involves increasing your *odds bet* as you make successive passes. The odds bet is the one you make after your point is determined by positioning the bet behind your pass-line bet. It's the only bet on the table that pays off at true odds as follows:

- Points 6 and 8 pay 6 to 5

- Points 5 and 9 pay 3 to 2

- Points 4 and 10 pay 2 to 1

It's called odds bet because you are taking the odds (and these are actual mathematical odds) that you will make your point. Please memorize the payoff numbers given here because you should always check your payoff by the dealer to ensure it's correct.

Again, the odds bet is an even bet with no built-in casino advantage, so it's an important part of our strategy because when we start even with the casino, the rhythm roll offers an even larger advantage.

See Exhibit 5, which illustrates the odds bet payoff (1) when your point is 6 or 8; (2) when your point is 5 or 9; and (3) when your point is 4 or 10.

Each of the following steps assumes successive pass-line wins. The essence of this pass-line strategy is to increase your bet one unit *after* each pass-line win—the increase, however, starts on the odds bet, not the pass-line bet. This up-as-you-win betting tactic exploits our advantage over the casino.

Step 1 and Step 2

Step 1: *Bet one unit on the pass line with no odds.* Step 2: *Bet one unit on the pass line; take the odds bet for one unit.*

Example. Bet $5 on the pass line and take the odds on 6 or 8, betting $5 to win $6.

If your point is 5 or 9, you bet $6 on the odds bet (always make your odds bet an even amount when the point is 5 or 9) to facilitate the 3-to-2 payoff. The reason is, if you bet $5 for example, your 3-to-2 win would equal $7.50 and the casino doesn't handle 50-cent pieces. So your odds bet is $6 to win $9. If your point is 4 or 10, take the odds bet for $5 to win $10.

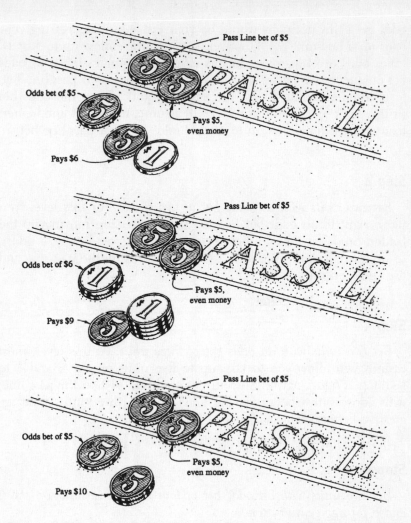

EXHIBIT 5: *Odds Bet Payoffs for points 6 or 8 (top); 5 or 9 (middle); 4 or 10 (bottom)*

Step 3

Bet one unit; take the odds for two units. Since most casinos allow *double odds* (allow you to take up to twice your pass-line bet as an odds bet), this normally would be your last step in increasing your odds on a one-unit bet. However, some casinos allow up to 5 or 10 times odds or even more. In this case, keep progressing your odds bet on successive passes, but only up to 5 times your pass-line bet, for example, betting $5 on the pass line and $25 as the odds bet (with $26 or $30 on the 5 or 9). I will assume, in Steps 4 and higher, that your casino allows up to double odds on your pass-line bet.

Step 4

Bet two units with an odds bet of two units. For this level, you move right to an odds bet to keep the progression moving up the ladder. Step 3 involved a bet of three units (1 pass line + 2 odds), so we move to four units at this step (two units on the pass line and two units on the odds bet).

Step 5

Bet two units with an odds bet of three units. At this level, most casinos will allow you to take up to five units on the 6 and 8 to facilitate a 6-to-5 payoff. So your bet could be $10 on the pass line, with conservative bettors taking odds of $15 (three units) and aggressive bettors taking $25 odds to win $30.

Step 6

Bet two units with an odds bet of four units (five units on the 6 and 8 for aggressive bettors).

Step 7

Bet three units with an odds bet of four units. Note that we are following our up-as-you-win strategy of increasing our bet by one unit overall, from six units in Step 6 to seven units in Step 7.

Step 8

Bet three units with an odds bet of five units.

Step 9

Bet three units with an odds bet of six units. Continue in this manner, progressing up to a four-unit pass-line bet.

In the heat of battle, if you get confused about where you are in the progression, keep it simple and don't worry if you miss a step or two. Just make the same size pass-line bet as the last one, take single odds, and go from there. If you forget your next step in the odds progression, just glance at the odds bet before the dealer pays you off. Notice the number of units and mentally add one to it; that's your next odds bet after the come-out roll establishes the point.

A note to conservative players: You don't have to raise your bet to get an advantage. Flat-betting is an accepted strategy when you've developed your rhythm roll. I would recommend, however, that if you flat-bet, take double odds.

BETTING TACTIC 2: PLACE BETTING THE 6 AND 8

The essence of this tactic is to flat-bet the 6 and 8 until you make your pass-line point; after every point is made, you increase your 6 and 8 place bets one unit. It's that simple.

Step 1

Place the 6 and 8 after the come-out roll for $6 each to win $7. If your point is the 6 or 8, just place the other one; for example, if your point is 6, place the 8. Collect on the 6 and 8 place bets for all times they hit. Continue collecting until you make your pass-line number or seven out.

Step 2

Increase your 6 and 8 place bets. This assumes you make your point and win your pass-line bet. After the next come-out roll, increase your 6 and 8 place bets one unit as follows:

If your new point is not 6 or 8, and the last point was 6 or 8, bet $6 on the one not covered—now you have $6 bet on each of the 6 and 8 and you are rolling for your new point.

But if your new point is a 6 or 8, leave your one place bet up and use it to cover the other number (if your pass line is 6, move your $6 bet to the 8, and vice versa). If you have bets on both the 6 and 8, which you probably will, take down the one that is not your number (if your point is 6, the jargon is "down on the 8 bet" and vice versa).

For this Step 2, you will *press* on the next hit. In craps jargon, to press means to double your bet; in this example, if 6 or 8 hits, double up your bet to $12. Your objective on this pass-line roll is to move up to a $12 bet on both the 6 and 8 or $12 on whichever one is not your point. When either the 6 or 8 hits, your instruction to the dealer is simply "Press." He will take $6 of your $7 payoff, reposition the bet to two $5 chips on the bottom and two $1 chips on top, and toss you the "change" of $1.

You have used your advantage to move to a two-unit pass-line bet; now you want to do the same with the 6 and 8 place bets.

Once you have achieved this objective, continue to collect $14 each time you roll a 6 or 8. Do not progress until after you make your pass-line point, as we will describe shortly.

Step 3

Continue to move your place bet up one unit as you make each pass-line number. That is, after you make two points (two pass-line wins), increase your bet from two units or $12 to three units or $18 on the next 6 or 8 hit after your third pass-line number is established. Sevens on the come-out roll do not count for increasing your place bets, only for establishing and then making your pass-line number.

Step 4

Let the next place-bet win on the 6 and/or 8 finance your next bet increase up to $24, or four units. To reach this step, you would have made three pass-line numbers; now you are working on your fourth. A possible point of confusion is when 6 or 8 is your point, winning the pass-line (making a pass-line number of 6 or 8), collecting on your pass-line win, and then throwing a non-six or -eight on your next come-out roll.

Let's say you're at Step 4, you make your point of 8, you have an $18 place bet on the 6, and you roll a 5 as your new point. How much do you place bet on the 8?

Conservative bettors should toss the dealer $6 and say, "Make my 6 place bet look like $12 each on the 6 and 8." The dealer takes $6 off your 6 place bet, combines it with the $6 you just tossed her, and places it on the 8. Sure, you're backing off a little, but that's okay. Keep it simple and keep your focus on your rhythm roll.

Aggressive bettors should place-bet the 8 for $18 and finance it out of their winnings accumulated up to Step 4. Another aggressive option for this betting tactic is to press the 6 and 8 on every other hit; for example, roll a 6 and win $7; roll another 6 and press your bet to $12; roll another 6 and win $14; roll another 6 and press to $24, and so forth. The 8 works the same way.

After you win a pass-line bet, there will be a little time available as the dealer pays off the other pass-line winners. Use this time to note your place bets and decide what to do on the next come-out roll. As you get experienced, this process should only take a few seconds. Then return to your focus on the rhythm roll.

You can also use this time to segregate your winnings into the back rack and, of course, decide on your next pass-line bet, with the odds you will take depending on the point rolled.

There are two "racks" or "rows" in front of you on the craps table. It is prudent to keep your buy-in chips in the front rack as "working capital" and move your winnings to the back rack. But, again, I stress not to get caught up in handling your chips and managing your money to the detriment of focusing on your next roll.

Notice how the other players organize their chips the next time you're at the craps table. Some do not organize at all, and you see a rainbow of white, red, green, and even black $100 chips all mixed together. Others carefully organize their chips by color; some segregate their winnings to the back rack. But don't spend too much time fiddling with your chips. Rhythm rolling and focus, not chip handling, is always your top priority; you can count your winnings after you seven out.

BETTING TACTIC 3: COVERING ALL THE NUMBERS

This tactic is for players with small bankrolls who want action on every roll.

As you become experienced with the rhythm roll, you will want all the numbers working for you — even the 2, 3, 11, and 12, which do not count after your point is established. The way to do this is to work with a *field bet*. The field bet is a one-roll bet that pays even money if you roll a 3, 4, 9, 10, or 11, and double on the 2 and 12. You win if any of these numbers are rolled on the next roll, and you lose on a non-field number: 5, 6, 8 and, of course, 7.

The tactic is to place the 5, 6, and 8 for two units ($10, $12, and $12) and play the field for one unit (which is $5 in our example). In this way, you win no matter what the outcome of the next roll is (except, of course, the losing 7). If the 5, 6, or 8 hit, you win $14 and lose your $5 field bet for a net win of $9. If the field hits, you win $5 (or $10 if the 2 or 12 is thrown), with your place bets not affected (they stay up until you take them down or the 7 is thrown). For this betting tactic, you have to bet the field on every roll because it is a one-roll bet.

This strategy is aggressive because you are risking $39 or just about eight betting units to win one or two ($5 on a field number, and $9 on a 5, 6, or 8). As long as your SRR is 7 or higher, however, you can afford to take the risk. Conservative players may wish to take their place bets down after four, five, or six rolls and stop betting the field. In this way you lock up your profits before the losing 7 shows. Aggressive bettors will use their profits to finance the other place bets—the 4, 9, and 10. The field bet would be terminated as these bets are made.

In this chapter, you have learned how to exploit your advantage by betting. In the next chapter, I discuss other ways to maintain and enhance your advantage.

Fourteen

HOW TO MAINTAIN AND IMPROVE YOUR CRAPS ADVANTAGE

The rhythm roll and set gives you an advantage over the casino by altering the natural outcome of the dice. Now that you have identified and learned to exploit this advantage, you need to maintain and even enhance it. Here are a few tips on how to accomplish this.

MAINTAIN YOUR ADVANTAGE

Tip 1

Never play with "scared money." Realize that you could lose. Find your comfort level. Don't chase losses. If your betting units are too high for your comfort level, this could affect your execution of the rhythm roll.

Tip 2

Do not let dealers or other players annoy you. If this is not possible, leave the table. Making dollar bets for the dealers on a hardway point or a come-out 11 will nullify any interference with your delivery or heat of any kind. Do not get caught up in the excitement of the game as the other players urge you on to make your point or numbers. Maintain focus. There will be plenty of time after your long roll to let the adrenaline flow, enjoy the win, and accept the kudos from the other players.

Tip 3

Try this approach to maintain your focus: When rolling, especially when the table gets crowded, try to find a "hallway" at the far end of the table with about a foot between two pass-line or odds bets as your target area. Then extend the hallway back to your spot. Then, just throw the dice down the hallway, trying to deaden them off the far wall. Picture a cereal bowl sitting against the end of the wall, and just try to lob the dice into the bowl—softly, so they'll stay in it.

Tip 4

Never play when you are depressed, tired, sick, or under the influence of alcohol. For the majority of players, alcohol has no part in a successful craps session. If you're a moderate drinker, be careful about playing craps after dinner. Sure, it's relaxing, but does it contribute to a better focus and therefore a more successful session? It may be the reverse—for some people, it may actually be more difficult or even impossible to focus after imbibing alcohol. However, some gamblers loosen up a bit after a cocktail or two, which allows them to focus better and execute a more accurate rhythm roll. Only you know your limits, so be careful.

Tip 5

If possible, warm up before your session. After arriving at the casino, get "grooved in" quickly by playing a few "hit-and-run" games wherever possible. When you seven out, leave the table and look for another one where you can get a shooting opportunity quickly. Don't let early seven outs discourage you! Remember, even though you have the edge, you have to "key it in" with muscle memory leading to your rhythm roll. Every one of us has a different set of muscles with a different muscle memory. Knowing yours is extremely important.

Tip 6

Never "show off" your power, such as by calling numbers before you throw or boasting to the other players about your advantage.

Tip 7

Do tip the dealers to get them on your side. It's just amazing how much cooperation a dollar or two bet will secure. Bet a dollar on the hard-way point you're shooting for, on the pass line, or on the seven on the come-out roll.

Tip 8

Don't stay too long or get too greedy at any one table or in any one casino. And, to avoid heat, never ever mention *rhythm roll*, *controlled throw*, or any similar terms on the casino floor or at the craps table.

Tip 9

Don't expect to win every time out. Even though you have an advantage, this doesn't mean that you'll always win.

Tip 10

Adopt a betting strategy in keeping with your aversion to risk—
start conservatively, maybe even flat-betting.

Tip 11

Always be on the lookout for other rhythm rollers. In the next
section, I'll show you how to find and exploit them.

HOW TO FIND AND EXPLOIT OTHER RHYTHM ROLLERS

Some shooters have perfected their throws to the level of actually
possessing an advantage. Others, throwing with a nice easy rhythm
without deviation from throw to throw, may not realize they have
an advantage. Also, sometimes their throw may deliver an advantage,
and sometimes not. Here's how to evaluate other shooters to discern
whether they are in the advantage zone.

First, watch to see whether they set the dice. Any set is better
than none as long as they don't set for the 7. Believe it or not, some
shooters set the dice with a 7 showing on one side and then attempt
to make their point. These are the types of shooters to consider
betting against.

Second, watch their throw. If they pick up the dice and throw
them the same way every time, with a nice, easy arc, this is a shooter
to consider betting on. Even if they don't set the dice, their rhythm
roll may deliver a small edge, except those throws where a 7 is
showing on the side. If they throw the dice randomly, so that they
bounce off the table, hard against the wall, or haphazardly come to
a stop anywhere on the table, do not risk any money on these shooters (or very little if you're playing recreationally). You may wish to
consider betting the don't-pass line. (Don't Pass is the opposite of
betting the pass line; you are betting that the shooter will throw a
7 before rolling his or her point.)

If the shooter exhibits any kind of control as described, use the conservative pass-line betting strategy described in Chapter 13. Consider moving to the place-bet strategy if the shooter shows signs of rolling a long hand. The keys are the parabolic arc and the consistency of the throw. Keep in mind that not all shooters who exhibit these characteristics will deliver an advantage. Go easy on your betting and make them prove it!

In this next section, I'll give you an example of a rhythm roller that I found and used to my advantage.

How to Use Another Rhythm Roller to Your Advantage

I was in the Hilton Casino in Atlantic City, observing a fairly crowded craps table, when the dice were passed to a young lady to my right. I figured she'd quickly seven out and I'd have the dice in no time, because she didn't look like much of a craps player.

I watched her roll a few numbers, including three 11s in four rolls. I decided to "tiptoe" into the game with a $10 come bet. She rolled a 6. I took single odds. She rolled a few more numbers. I won the 6, so I proceeded to load up on three more $10 come bets.

Now she had my attention. She had a funny way of cupping her right hand over the dice and jiggling them a little bit on the table surface before setting and then throwing them with a nice, clean, medium-arced throw down into the left-hand corner of the table. A rhythm roller. I became convinced when she rolled a couple of more points with a few numbers in between.

Now my pass-line bet is up to my standard $30 unit and I've loaded up three $30 come bets, all with double odds.

She goes through the same routine every time, sets the dice the same way every time, and is throwing number after number.

I get worried when the cocktail waitress bothers her with her drink order; she turns around to tip the waitress and I wonder if I should take my odds bets down—is her rhythm broken? No. She nonchalantly returns to the task at hand and continues throwing numbers.

I've now got $30 on the pass-line with odds of $60. Her point is 4. She makes the 4 and I pick up my win of $150 ($30 from the pass-line win and $120 from the double-odds win). I leave $30 on the pass line for the next come-out roll. My last come bet—$30—goes to the 4. I throw the dealer $60 for the odds on this last come bet and say, "Let it work." On the come-out roll, all odds bets are automatically turned off because the players are all pulling for the winning 7 on this come-out roll. This means that if the shooter should throw another 4 on the come-out roll, that $60 odds bet would not win $120. You have to tell the dealer that the bet "works." Since I was already on the 4, that bet pays off but stays up because the last number rolled was a 4.

On the come-out roll she rolls a 6, so I position $100 behind the $30 pass-line bet for the odds. I make another $30 come bet and watch her roll another 4. Off and on for $150 ($30 pays $30; $60 pays $120 with the 2-to-1 odds). This means that my come bet stays on the 4. I watch in amazement as she rolls two more 4s in succession, and I win $150 on each one.

However, this young lady is making $5 and $10 bets and not raising her bet. She's now been throwing the dice for 20 minutes or so (remember, it was a crowded table) and she's won only about $50. Every so often she complains to the dealer that nobody is betting for her! She's casting envious glances at the black and green chips that many of the other players are accumulating and wishing she had some. This tells me she is a novice at the game, that she has a natural rhythm roll and does not know how to exploit it to her advantage.

She continues to roll, but her numbers include more 4s, even some the hard way, and more 11s than any one shooter should be allowed. The only 7s she throws are two—on the come-out roll (wiping out my three come bets—by this time $50 with double odds). But this doesn't even bother me and I proceed to load up again and continue taking down profits.

When she finally sevened out, 45 minutes after I entered the game, I left about $600 on the table between my pass-line loss and three come bets lost. But I had taken down over $2,000 in profits on this incredible roll, even with betting very conservatively (for me) by starting with a $10 bet and incrementing by only $10 on every other win (bet $10, win, bet $10, win, now bet $20). My last bet was $50 with full double odds.

An interesting footnote to the story—I had my best roll of the session when I got the dice after her roll, feeling really grooved in, and picked up another $500 in about a 10-to-15-minute shoot. When I sevened out, I drew a few boos, whereas the young lady had received a boisterous round of applause. Such are the caprices of craps players.

The message in this case study is simple: Always be on the lookout for other rhythm rollers, but evaluate them carefully before committing big money to their hand.

If you're just gambling for fun and don't wish to get involved evaluating other shooters, you could still use any of the three betting tactics described in Chapter 13, depending on the degree of risk you wish to take. Use one of these betting tactics even if you are not executing a rhythm roll.

WHERE TO GO FROM HERE

I've given you enough information and instruction in this chapter to use your rhythm roll to your advantage and to identify other shooters who possess this skill. Your next step after reading this book is to practice your rhythm roll at home. Record each throw and see how long you can continue throwing before the seven shows. Then compute your seven-to-rolls ratio (divide your total number of throws by the number of sevens thrown). Use the graph in Chapter 11, Exhibit 4, to determine your advantage. If you are interested in further instruction on controlled throws and would like to network with other rhythm rollers, I invite your inquiry about our instructional program called "Sharpshooter Craps." We don't offer it to the public—only to readers of my books who get to know us and whom we get to know. Use the coupon in the back of this book to request detailed information.

Section Four

ROULETTE

Fifteen

BASIC ROULETTE

HISTORY

Although the precise origin of roulette—the oldest casino game still in existence—appears to be lost in antiquity, there's ample evidence that men have gambled by spinning wheels for centuries. Ancient warriors whirled shields on the tips of their swords, and Romans turned over chariots to spin the wheels on their axles. The invention of roulette (from the French word *roue*, meaning "wheel") has been attributed variously to prehistoric Chinese, to French monks, to an Italian mathematician identified only as Don Pasquale, and to a brilliant seventeenth-century French scientist, Blaise Pascal. In all likelihood, roulette simply evolved from other games of chance.

In 1765, a police official, Gabriel de Sartine, who wanted a gambling game that would thwart the cheats then plaguing the city, introduced the present form of roulette in Paris. Its acceptance was almost instantaneous, and its popularity in France continues to this day. Just a little earlier, in 1739, a similar game called E-O (for even-odd) was first played in the city of Bath, England. However, the game became obsolete by about 1820, when refugees from the French Revolution introduced roulette, with its greater variety of bets.

Early nineteenth-century roulette had both a single and double zero, very much like the wheels used in Las Vegas today. When the ball dropped into the red single 0, all bets on red were considered *bars*, and no money was won or lost. Conversely, when the ball landed in the black 00 pocket, all bets on black were barred. Interestingly, the same principle and terminology are used today in casino craps with its Don't Pass Bar 12 line.

The single-zero wheel so prevalent in Europe today was introduced in 1842 by Francois and Louis Blanc. Both men left France to operate a casino in Hamburg, Bavaria, because gambling had become illegal. Their new wheel, which cut the house edge from 5.26 to 2.70 percent, decimated the competition, as the Blanc brothers had correctly forecast that reducing the odds would increase the attractiveness of the game and ultimately result in greater profits. After his brother died, Francois Blanc accepted an invitation from the Prince of Monaco, Charles III (for whom Monte Carlo is named), to purchase a franchise to operate his opulent new casino for nearly two million francs. The Blancs' roulette quickly became the most popular game, particularly with the social elite. Gambling was still outlawed in France, and Monsieur Blanc, referred to as the "most brilliant financier of his time" by Lord Brougham, high chancellor of England, successfully financed the opposition to legalized casinos in Italy. Along with his son Camille, Francois Blanc (who left a fortune of 200 million francs) operated Monte Carlo for nearly 65 years; this father and son are credited for its development into the world-famous resort it is today.

Roulette Emigrates to the United States

Roulette came to the United States in the early 1800s, landing first in New Orleans. The wheel in use had both the single and double zeros, but the operators, lacking the wisdom of the Blanc brothers, added rather than subtracted a zero. This third zero position featured a picture of an American eagle and tripled the house percentage over the single-zero game. Still not content, the operators increased the speed of the wheel to three times the pace of the leisurely 36 spins per hour of the game played in the European casinos. In the noisy and smoky casinos and saloons of the Old West, roulette competed equally with poker, faro, dice, dog fighting, and other games of chance for the gamblers' money.

This is in marked contrast to how roulette was perceived in Europe. It was, and still is, considered to be an elegant game favored by the rich and commoners alike — especially women, who seem to appreciate the sophisticated environment of subdued glamour and relative simplicity of the game, although the action, in reality, is quite fast. Roulette is one of the most popular gambling games in Europe, especially in Monte Carlo.

However, roulette never quite reached the same level of acceptance in the United States. When legalized gambling first emerged in the 1930s — and even in the preceding two or three decades, when illegal gambling was available at posh spas from Saratoga, New York, to Palm Beach, Florida — roulette received more than its fair share of play. However, after World War II, it was surpassed by craps, and subsequently both were eclipsed by blackjack.

With the introduction of the European option of *en prison* or *surrender* for the outside even-money bets (see the next section for a definition), roulette seems to be now holding its own in the many new casinos opening in the United States.

TODAY'S GAME

Most roulette games today are played with double-zero wheels. Single-zero wheels can be found at some of the larger casinos, but with a higher betting minimum. Some casino locations feature "surrender" for the outside even-money bets. This means that if a zero or double zero hits, half the bet is returned to the player. The term *surrender* comes from the European game, which features an *en prison* rule for even-money bets, meaning that the bet is moved to the side, or put "in prison," when the zero hits, until the next roll. If the player's bet wins on that next spin, the bet is now whole again and is moved "out of prison" and back to the regular spot in the betting square. The effect is that half the bet is lost or "surrendered" on the zero or double zero.

This bet reduces the house edge to 2.63 percent on even-money bets and is more favorable on the European single-zero wheels, as it reduces the casino edge to just 1.3 percent on the outside bets.

Basic Rules of Play

Before you can play, you must purchase special roulette chips, which are different from those used in other areas of the casino. Roulette chips can be obtained in stacks of 20 from the *croupier* with either money or regular casino chips, and they can't be used or exchanged anywhere else in the casino. Each table has its own supply of six or seven distinctly colored chips in sets of 300, one color for each player, and no one else can use this color until the player leaves the table. At this time, he or she must surrender them for regular casino chips, which can be converted into currency at the cashier's station. These roulette chips have no monetary value printed on them. Each buyer declares their value when he or she purchases them, and the croupier places a numbered marker on the table's supply to indicate their value, which can be any amount from 50 cents up to the table maximum. In actual practice they are rarely valued above $25.

The roulette layout allows only one spot to place a bet, so it is likely that more than one person will bet on the same number. If someone has bet on the number you wish to bet on, you simply place your chips on top of the other player's. Because of the different colors, the croupier can easily keep track of each player's chips, eliminating any possible dispute between two players claiming the same bet. This American innovation is a distinct improvement over the European game, where there are frequent arguments over who placed which bet.

Once you have a stack of chips and understand all about minimum bets (see page 159), pick a lucky number or spot, place some chips on the layout, and watch the ball spin around the turning wheel. When the ball stops, the croupier will mark the winning

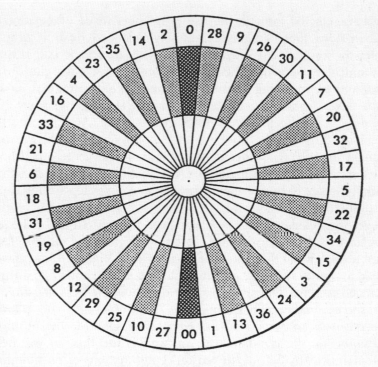

FIGURE 9: *The Double-Zero American Roulette Wheel*

number, remove all the losing bets, and leave the winning wagers, which he then pays off. Players can now make new bets, and may continue to place chips on the layout until a few seconds before the ball is about to drop, at which time the croupier announces, "No more bets." Any bets placed after this announcement are returned to the player, whether they win or lose.

THE WHEEL

The following description is based on the double-zero American roulette wheel, shown in Figure 9.

The game of roulette is based on a random choice of one of 38 numbers selected through the use of a wheel made of a stationary 32-inch bowl that contains a precisely balanced rotating 24-inch center section called a *wheel head*. A nylon or acetate ball is spun by the dealer in a clockwise direction around the outer rim of the bowl, and after circling a number of times, the whirling ball slowly drops down toward the center, frequently striking the silver diamond-shaped deflectors embedded in the apron. As it reaches the wheel head, which is turning in the opposite direction, the ball bounces around a number of times among the vertical partitions that separate the 38 numbered red, black, and green pockets before it finally settles in one of them, thereby selecting the winning number and color.

The 38 pockets, which are alternately colored red and black except for the green zeros, appear to be numbered in a random fashion, but that is not the case. As far as possible, high and low as well as odd and even numbers are alternately spaced in a mathematically balanced pattern. The single zero and the double zero are directly opposite each other, and 1 is opposite 2, 3 is opposite 4 and so forth. The numbers and colors on the wheel correspond to the numbers and colors on the layout. Once you understand this, all you need now is an explanation of the various combinations of possible bets and their odds.

Table Layout

To the novice player, the layout looks formidable, but the game is really quite easy to learn. The main section is composed of 36 red and black boxes numbered in sequence from top to bottom and arranged in three columns of 12 spaces each. At the head of the columns, numbered 1, 2, and 3, are two more oddly shaped green spaces for the zeros. At the foot of these columns are three spaces marked "2 to 1." A bet placed in one of these indicates you are betting on all the numbers in the column above. Directly along the front side of the columns are three boxes marked "1st 12," "2nd 12," and "3rd 12." A bet placed in the first of these indicates you are betting on all the numbers 1 through 12, a bet in the second would

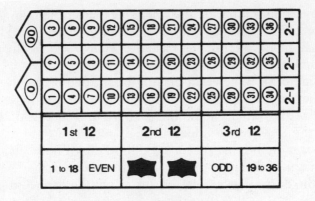

FIGURE 10: *Roulette Table Layout*

cover 13 through 24, and in the third it would cover 25 through 36. Just in front of these three are six more spots for wagers on numbers 1 through 18, all even numbers, all red spots, all black spots, all odd numbers, and the numbers 19 through 36. You must be careful that your chips are placed precisely where you want to bet. If you can't reach a spot, slide your chips toward the croupier and tell him where to place them.

With only eleven possible wagers divided into just two types, betting rules are easily learned. Refer to Figure 10 as you read the descriptions of the various bet types.

Types of Bets

All roulette tables have two minimum bets: one for the even-money and 2-to-1 wagers, called the *outside bets*, and another for the number wagers, called the *inside bets*. For example, at a $5 table the minimum value of the colored chips would be $1, and one outside bet must be for at least five chips; other outside bets made at the same time can be for as little as one chip. Inside bets can also be for as little as one chip as long as the player has a total of at least five chips on the inside layout for the roll. There is no limit to the number of bets that can be made, although the casino does have a maximum limit for any single bet. This maximum is usually $100 for each inside bet, $500 for each 2-to-1 bet, and $1,000 for each even-money bet. Bigger casino operators will frequently raise these limits for high-rolling bettors.

Outside Bets. When you place a bet in one of the three boxes at the bottom of the number columns, you are making a column bet and betting on all the numbers above it; if successful, you'll be paid at the 2-to-1 rate printed in these spots.

To wager on the first, second, and third dozen numbers, put your chips in one of the appropriate boxes. If any one of the 12 numbers within the dozen you've selected shows up, the bank also pays 2 to 1.

For a bet on all 18 low numbers or all 18 high numbers (a high bet or a low bet), merely set some chips in one of these two boxes. You will get even money if you win.

Chips placed in either the even or the odd box cover all 18 corresponding numbers, and winners are again paid even money. To make a bet on all the red or black numbers, set some chips in the designated box for another possible even-money payoff.

In some casinos the player only loses half his bet on even-money bets, which reduces the house edge to 2.63 percent.

Inside Bets. There are six types of inside bets on the numbers or combinations of numbers. To make the single-number inside bet (called *straight up*), simply place your chips on any one of the 38 numbered squares, including the zeros, being careful that your bet does not touch any line. If the ball lands in the corresponding numbered pocket on the next spin, you win and the bank pays off at 35 to 1. Remember that your original bet stays on the layout and rides on the next spin unless you pick it up. True odds would have been 37 to 1; consequently, the house advantage is 5.26 percent. This edge is constant for all bets in the double-zero game, with the exception of the five-number bet covered later. When you find a single-zero game, the casino edge is reduced to 2.70 percent.

If you want to bet on either of two adjoining numbers on the layout (called a *split bet*), put your wager directly on the line separating them. If one of them wins, you are paid off at 17 to 1. There are 62 possible two-number bets.

For a *three-number bet*, set your chip or chips on the line at the bottom (closest to you) of any of the 12 rows of three numbers or at the junction of the 0, 00, and 2 squares; the 0, 1, and 2 squares; or the 00, 2, and 3 squares. This adds up to 15 available three-number bets, and the payoff is 11 to 1.

A chip placed at the intersection of any four numbers is called a *corner bet*. There are 22 of these, and if any one of the four numbers comes up, you are paid 8 to 1.

The only possible *five-number bet* is on the line between the zeros and 1, 2, and 3 at the intersection with the 1st-12 square. Of course, this bet is not available in a single-zero game. In the double-zero game, it's the worst bet on the table, paying 6 to 1, with the casino advantage jumping to 7.89 percent.

You can make a *six-number* bet on the junction formed by the line dividing any two rows of three numbers where it intersects with the Dozen box. The bank pays 5 to 1 if you bet on one of these eleven combinations and any one of the six numbers is spun.

THE LURE OF UP-AS-YOU-LOSE SYSTEMS

Martingale, D'Alembert, Labouchere, Fibonacci — all exotic names describing betting systems usually associated with roulette or craps and having one characteristic in common: Each involves betting up as you lose on even-money bets, such as red or black at roulette or don't-pass at craps. The only difference is when and how much.

Martingale advises doubling up after each loss until a win. At that point you're one unit ahead.

D'Alembert's method involves upping a unit on a loss and reducing a unit on a win.

Labouchere's system is based on cancellation. The player writes down a series of numbers, such as 1-2-3-4, and then bets the sum of the two outside numbers. On a loss, the amount just bet is added to the series; on a win, the two outside numbers are canceled. The objective is to cancel out the series, thereby taking down the sum of the series numbers as a win—for example, 10 units in our example. The theory is that, since you are canceling two numbers on a win and writing down only one number on a loss, you can win money by winning less than half of your bets.

The Fibonacci series, upon which the betting system is based, is quite simple: 1, 2, 3, 5, 8, 13, and so on. Each series number is the sum of the prior two. Using this system, you start with the smallest number and move up one level each time you lose. When you win, you move down a level and bet that number. Your objective is to win two bets in succession or two out of three; then you start over.

Each of these systems has been around for more than 100 years, and they don't even represent the current state of the art. However, they are still around, and are usually the first systems a beginning roulette player tries out. These systems are repackaged every few years with a new wrinkle or two to make them look different and new. You may find them in a "new" book, offered for sale on the Internet, or in a sales letter mailed to unsuspecting gamblers. They are touted as unbeatable and the key to fabulous riches. "Just send me $25" (or higher but usually no more than $100), the system seller asks. "If it doesn't work, send it back and I'll refund your money."

The major problem with these systems is that you are risking your entire bankroll to win a single unit, as with Martingale and D'Alembert, or just a few units, as with Labouchere and Fibonacci. But the systems are attractive to neophyte gamblers because they actually win a majority of the time. With the Martingale system, for example, the casino would have to beat you eight times in succession to wipe out your 25-unit bankroll. "Impossible," the system seller says. But if you play long enough, you will suffer the inevitable wipeout series. In the meantime, you're "dancing among the raindrops," but you can't avoid getting wet forever. It's just a matter of time.

UP-AS-YOU-WIN SYSTEMS

If you're a recreational gambler, I suggest you consider using an up-as-you-win system, such as "Oscar's Grind" or "Reverse Labouchere."

Oscar's Grind

With Oscar's Grind, the first bet is one unit; you continue betting one unit on successive losses. The bet is increased by one unit on a win and stays at that level until another win; that is, the player continues betting two units until another win, then increases subject to the condition described in a moment. The objective is to clear a profit of one unit on each series. Therefore, your bets later in the series will not relate to prior bets. As the series progresses, the next bet following a win is defined as just enough to recoup all prior losses plus a one-unit profit. You can find a fascinating description, workout, and history of Oscar's Grind in Allan Wilson's classic book *The Casino Gambler's Guide* (Harper & Row, 1970).

Reverse Labouchere

Many gamblers will recognize the Reverse Labouchere system as the one used by the roulette team for their big score at Monte Carlo in the book *Thirteen Against the Bank* (Morrow, 1976). The strategy is to add numbers to the series on wins instead of on losses. Let the series run and bets continue to increase until the house limit, or a predefined maximum bet, is reached. There is one catch to using this system in U.S. casinos, and that is the minimum bet size—to cover lots of crossed-out losing series, you need one as small as possible while waiting for your big score. The players in *Thirteen Against the Bank* enjoyed a minimum bet around 25 cents; over here it's usually between $1 and $5, so be careful!

Sixteen

STATE-of-the-ART ADVANTAGE ROULETTE SYSTEMS

Six authors have identified and published advantage methods for beating the wheel and gaining an edge over the house. These methods represent the current state of the art in roulette advantage systems. Their methods can be classified into three types:

Type 1: Biased-wheel methods

Type 2: Prediction methods

Type 3: Dealer-signature methods

BIASED-WHEEL METHODS

In his book *The Casino Gambler's Guide* (Harper & Row, 1965), Allan Wilson discussed his approach for detecting and exploiting biased roulette wheels. He defined biased wheels as those that contain some kind of mechanical flaw that contributes to a non-random distribution of numbers being rolled. In months of searching and after documenting tens of thousands of spins, he found one in Reno,

Nevada, with a small bias. He and a friend played it for scores of hours and eventually turned a small profit.

In today's high-tech world, biased roulette wheels are rare if not impossible to find, but Wilson's theories were interesting at the time and encouraged others to do further research. In the late 1980s, most casinos changed their wheels to a style far less susceptible to mechanical biases. Biased-wheel play, for all practical purposes, died when that happened.

Russell Barnhart documented an interesting history of biased wheels in his fine book *Beating the Wheel* (Lyle Stuart, 1992). His biased-wheel chapters are interesting reading, but no help in today's casino environment.

PREDICTION METHODS

Concealed computers were the subjects of intense research in the 1980s. Thomas Bass designed a hidden computer that, with two points of wheel reference input, calculated the decaying orbit of the ball as it slowed and descended into a pocket. Using this information, the computer predicted the sector of the wheel into which the ball would fall. Theoretically, and in the laboratory, the method worked quite well; you can read a fascinating account in his book *The Eudaemonic Pie* (Vintage Books, 1986). However, the computer failed miserably in real-world casino action. Logistics, human observation and communication errors, electronic glitches, and a host of other foul-ups all contributed to insurmountable problems.

Scott Lang self-published a book called *Beat Roulette with a Patented New Discovery: Target Sectoring the Queen of Gambling Games* (Whirling Lady Press, 1983). This method yielded a mathematical advantage and I was excited enough to purchase a casino-quality roulette wheel.

The method depended on timing the wheel with the click of a stopwatch as the ball passed the zero point and another click at the same reference point two revolutions later. The elapsed time for two revolutions was plugged into a memorized table of sectors, and the numbers in the appropriate sector were bet either straight up or in pairs.

I and a number of my students enjoyed a modest success in casino play until the casinos caught on. The method depended on a slowly spinning wheel — two seconds or more per revolution, so the casinos simply increased the speed of the wheels and our advantage was eliminated.

Lawrence Scott developed a visual method for clocking the wheel and published it as a complete learning kit that included a video called *How to Beat Roulette*. Even at the steep price of $295, he sold quite a few. People such as Stanford Wong and Arnold Snyder evaluated the method and gave it a positive rating in their newsletters.

But everyone, including Scott himself, recognized the difficulties of learning the visual prediction method and applying it under actual casino conditions. To start with, you have to watch a ball spinning around a wheel, estimate the velocity, and then mentally calculate where it's going to fall. It's just too cumbersome to apply for most gamblers, even serious ones. There are only a handful of players using it today, including my associate Sharpshooter worked directly with Scott, assisting him with fine-tuning and validating the visual prediction method.

If there are, in fact, a handful of players using visual methods to clock wheels or find biased wheels, John Julian will show you how to find them and cap their bets in his book *The Julian Strategies on Roulette* (Paone Press, 1992). Frank Scoblete summarizes Julian's method as a 10-step process and calls it the Chameleon Strategy in his book *Spin Roulette Gold* (Bonus Books, 1997).

If you find a player using a visual method, Scoblete says to play him for 20 spins and, if you're ahead, keep playing; if you're behind, maybe he isn't really an advantage player and you should cease, move on, and find another one. If you employ the Julian strategy, be careful; it might be just pure luck, and you'll be gambling right along with him and playing into the casino's 5 percent-plus edge.

DEALER-SIGNATURE METHODS

Now we come to the dealer as the prediction factor and discuss *dealer signatures*. A signature is a predictable pattern the dealer uses—in most case unconsciously—to spin the wheel.

But do dealer signatures really exist? Will a dealer get into a rhythm, a groove, when picking up the ball and releasing it? Will the release be similar or the same? Will the velocity be the same? Is muscle memory involved in the dealer's spinning and release process to make it sort of automatic? We'll answer these questions in the pages that follow.

Our state-of-the-art assessment of signature methods revealed that it's possible for dealers to develop enough skill to aim for a specific sector of the wheel.

My associate Eric Nielsen observed countless games and interviewed dozens of pit personnel, and has concluded that at least 20 percent of all active roulette dealers are skilled enough to consciously direct the ball into a specific wheel sector. He once had a dealer demonstrate exactly how he did it. In his demonstration, the dealer "aimed" at the number 5 and hit it dead-on in 3 out of 10 attempts! Most books on roulette refute this assertion, as do the scientists and mathematical types who are more comfortable with visual prediction methods. Don't believe them for a moment. If you have any doubts, simply spend a day watching the wheels—you will quickly become a believer.

Frank Scoblete, in his book *Spin Roulette Gold,* says that there may be signatures and suggests the possibility that they can be used to predict the sector into which the ball will fall. He presents a somewhat "brute force" method for finding the signature by documenting the relative numbers for the dealer whose signature you are attempting to determine. He defines an arbitrary number of spins for the signature determination and gives no degree of confidence for the resulting signature. The player's judgment is used. Then, once you find the signature, you are betting, on the average, 11 numbers per spin. He recommends departure after three consecutive spins without a win and then trying it again with another dealer.

How We Developed Our Advantage Method

In early 1990, we began collecting sample spin results from roulette dealers in the Atlantic City casinos. Our analysis of this data led to the hypothesis that short-term random biases do, indeed, exist. Our detection of short-term random biases and continued observance and analysis of them in other casino locations was of little practical use, but it did spark our interest to continue our research and look further.

During the next six months, we studied most available literature on roulette and tested several hypotheses in actual casino trials. By late 1990, we were certain we had identified the reasons for these biases and, better yet, devised a simple "counting" method to track them, study them, and hopefully predict them. In the next four years we spent countless hours in and out of the casinos studying and testing dozens of approaches to exploiting the biases. In mid-summer 1994, we completed the development of our first fully validated method that yielded a positive advantage.

During the last quarter of 1993, we taught several advanced players our method, and they had little difficulty duplicating our results. Once we verified this correct path in our research, enhancements came quickly, and now we have successfully developed a number of winning approaches that yield profits even with a flat-betting approach—proof that our methods yield an advantage over the casino.

Shortly after beginning our research, we learned that the biases we observed were clearly caused by the dealer's influence on each spin of the wheel. Whether by conscious or subconscious action, each spin result is, in fact, highly influenced by this human element in casino roulette.

We became certain the dealers influence the game, but most do it in a subconscious fashion. They tend to repeat their "technique" over and over again, forming predictable patterns—or signatures. This theory is based on the fact that roulette is a highly mechanical game. If the wheel were to rotate at the same speed and the dealer were to release the ball precisely the same way for each spin, we could predict the sector into which the ball would drop quite frequently—certainly enough to get a huge edge over the casino. The fluctuation in wheel speed, dealer release technique, and *canoes* (deflector ball stops) create a more random outcome. Most dealers tend to repeat near-identical conditions in many of their spins—not consciously, but due largely to rote, repetition, or muscle memory—which create the bias, or dealer signature.

Many dealers, no matter how skilled they are or how hard they may try to "mix it up," will to some degree fall into this repetition and form a clear signature that can be exploited.

A dealer signature will usually be characterized by one of two identities:

1. Occurring around a relative number—for example, relative 17, which means that the predicted sector will be around 17 pockets away from the last hit.

2. Occurring in one specific sector of the wheel—for example, the contiguous pockets 7, 11, 30, 26, and 9. Once identified, these numbers would be bet on each spin until the signature changes.

The first method, using relative numbers for identification, is beyond the scope of this book. However interested readers and serious roulette players can use the framework approach presented in the remainder of this chapter for identifying dealer signatures characterized by relative numbers and, thus, prove to themselves that these types of dealer signatures do, in fact, exist.

The advantage method presented in the next chapter detects and exploits dealer signatures in the second category. It's called the Power Sector Method and, although less powerful than the relative number signature method, will be easy to learn and use by serious players as well as recreational players.

FACTORS INVOLVED IN ADVANTAGE PLAY

If you're a roulette enthusiast and want to play around with signatures characterized by relative numbers, document 25–50 spins of a single dealer on a roulette wheel by writing down the numbers as they hit. Then, at home, or up in your room, convert the spin results to relative numbers (a relative number is the number of pockets betwen two successive hits; see "How to Determine Relative Numbers" later in this chapter for detailed discussion). Study the resulting pattern. If you find one relative number occurring more often than the others, or three relative numbers occurring in a sequence like 16, 17, 18, you just might be looking at a dealer signature!

You can determine your advantage by examining 5-pocket sectors around the center of your signature; i.e. 17 in the above example. One of the five numbers in the 5-pocket sector defined by relative 17 (with relative 17 in the center and two numbers on either side) should hit about once every 7.6 spins on average. If these five numbers are hitting more often, say once every five spins, you have an advantage over this dealer. To exploit your advantage, you would bet one unit on each of the five numbers. (See "Placing Your Bets" on page 174 for more instructions.)

I must caution you, however, that this is just one example—space limitations prevent me from giving you specific relative number signature validation procedures for the many scenarios which may occur.

Study the remainder of this chapter carefully before you undertake this project. Do not bet to your possible relative number signature for the dealer you have documented unless you have a clear advantage.

Toking

In casino roulette, it is imperative to have the dealer on your side! Remember, talented dealers can effectively avoid your numbers if they wish. In the United States, dealers work for tokes (tips). Tokes account for a major portion of their paychecks. Hence, the most effective way to a dealer's heart is by way of toking. The way we toke in with the Power Sector Method (see Chapter 17) is by placing units on key numbers "for the dealers"—thus encouraging him or her to hit the number(s) we desire and ultimately win a nice toke. Remember, when we place a $1 chip on a number "straight up" "for the dealers" and the number hits, the dealers win $36! After a while you will become amazed at how often the dealers hit their numbers.

Dealer Selection

Before investing time studying dealers, it is helpful to prequalify them. Generally, the best dealers are those that exhibit consistency in their technique. The best dealers have the following characteristics:

- They have the same ball pickup and release technique on every spin.

- They maintain slow to moderate wheel speed.

- They are female, because female dealers tend to be less "combatant" compared to male dealers.

- They are relief dealers, because they move quickly from table to table and tend to be less protective of their territory.

- They are pit personnel doubling as dealers, because pit personnel, when asked to deal, tend to focus more on accurate and efficient table proceedings than on "mixing up" their spins.

The worst dealers display these characteristics:

- Their ball pickup and release technique is erratic.

- They hold out the ball excessively between spins.

- They clearly have bad attitudes.

- They maintain a very fast wheel speed.

- They maintain a very fast game speed (over 100 spins per hour).

You can effectively prequalify a dealer by watching just four or five spins. You will find that most dealers (about 75 percent) exhibit positive characteristics.

Table Conditions

Signatures will be strongest when the tables are moderately full (three or four players) to full (six or seven players). Generally, playing (or *charting*) when a table is relatively empty (one or two players) produces the least productive results. Also, when playing, you need 45 seconds between spins to play comfortably. Do not try to play in a game that is simply too fast. You cannot possibly maintain effective control. Each player will develop his or her own "speed threshold."

Game Departure

There are two departure factors you must observe. The first is *draw down* (losing activity), and the other is changing conditions.

Draw Down. If you find yourself drawn down 30 units from any high point in a particular game, you must consider leaving the game. Something is not working. Unless you see some strong positive indicators, leave now.

An easy way to monitor draw down is to buy in for 50 units and put 30 units into play, setting the remaining 20 aside. Maintain your play stack at 30 units. Whenever the play stack exceeds 50, put the excess in your aside stack. If you find your play stack gone, you are drawn down 30 units from high point. Needless to say, you do not have to wait for a 30-unit draw down to depart. You should realize, however, that even in a good game you could go five, six, or seven consecutive spins without a hit.

Changing Conditions. If you find that conditions change significantly at some point in your game, you should consider immediate departure. Significant changes can include the following:

- a ball change
- the game speeds up beyond playability
- the dealer becomes "combative" or irritable, or there is an obvious change in attitude
- the pit boss instructs the dealer to "mix it up"
- the dealer becomes obviously erratic with wheel speed or release technique
- wheel speed remains excessively fast

If a condition change is questionable, then simply sit out a couple of spins and see whether things return to normal.

Placing Your Bets

It is helpful to prepare several stacks of five chips in advance. That way, you can simply grab a stack and place the bets accordingly. When the hand is empty, that means all five numbers are covered. If you have leftover chips, you missed something. You should also ask the dealer to place some of your bets you cannot reach from your table position if you have only a limited time to get the bets down.

If you were to play perfectly (in theory), you would wait to witness a clean pickup and release before placing your bets, but usually you do not have the luxury of time. You must start laying your bets as soon as you have referenced your play numbers. A good dealer will give 80 percent consistency, and even on the 20 percent inconsistent releases, you have a full 32 percent chance of getting a random hit.

Wheel Styles

There are two primary wheel styles used in American casinos: those with *high-profile separators* and those with *low-profile* or *shallow separators*. The separators are also known as *frets*. Several specific manufacturers and models exist, but all fall under these two primary styles. Wheels with high frets tend to generate less bounce before the ball drops and give a stronger, more consistent signature. Wheels with low (shallow) frets are designed to produce a more random game by generating maximum ball bounce. Low-fret wheels are not as strong as high-fret wheels, but are still plenty good enough to beat. Remember, it is the dealer you are exploiting, not the wheel. However, given a choice, you should always pick a high-fret wheel.

Some casinos use clear plastic covers that only cover 300° of the wheel to keep the ball from flying out (60° is left open, obviously, to toss the ball in). Dealers believe that with these covers, they can spin the wheel to very fast speeds (creating a more random game) without having the ball fly out every spin. But because dealers have only a 60° opening to work through, they don't spin the wheel any faster and are forced to throw with greater consistency. These covers obviously give us an added advantage.

How to Determine Relative Numbers

Use a roulette scorecard illustration of the wheel. Here are three helpful hints to enhance your efficiency:

1. When you look at the illustration, always orient the wheel in the same fashion. I always position pocket 5 at 6:00. In no time, you will develop an automatic sense of where each number is positioned and be able to locate and count very quickly.

2. With the American wheel, there exists a constant relationship between any odd number and the even number that sequentially follows: 1 to 2, 3 to 4, 7 to 8, 25 to 26, 33 to 34, and so on. That relationship is 19. The distance from pocket 1 to

pocket 2 is 19 relative pockets (also exactly 180 across the wheel). Familiarize yourself with this and it will save considerable time in many instances. Remember that it works only when you start at the odd number in the pair.

3. In some cases it is much easier and faster to count backward to determine a relative number. Say we want to determine the relative number between 4 and 6. If we were to count clockwise, it would take a few extra seconds. Try counting backward, it will be much quicker. When counting backward, define your starting pocket as 38. Try a few examples; you will see it is quite easy and accurate.

Erroneous Wheel Illustrations. Beware! We frequently see wheel illustrations printed backward. In many casino books, and even on current casino scorecards, we find the pocket number sequences laid out in the wrong direction. If you use a bad illustration to determine relative numbers, you will naturally find yourself way off the mark when it comes time to play. It may also be possible that you will occasionally run across an actual wheel with its pocket numbering sequence laid out backward. If you are in unfamiliar territory, a quick check would be advised.

The proper sequence on an illustration or actual wheel may be verified by simply finding the single zero on the wheel, then looking from the outside of the wheel to the inside. Pocket 28 should always be the first pocket clockwise from the single zero. This is a simple rule. Commit it to memory and it will occasionally save you some unnecessary grief.

A note to the recreational player: After reading about the Power Sector Method in the next chapter, if you decide you don't want to take the time to master its execution, I suggest you try out a few of the simpler ideas described at the conclusion of the chapter.

A note to the serious player: Further instruction on relative number signature methods is available via the author's roulette instructors. Details can be found in the appendix.

Seventeen

THE POWER SECTOR METHOD
FOR ADVANTAGE ROULETTE

In the game of casino roulette, the dealer maintains significant influence over each and every spin result. Some dealers create biases by consciously attempting to hit certain numbers or sectors. Others create biases in a more subconscious manner through muscle memory.

The Power Sector Method is designed to exploit the bias created by certain dealers. Power Sector dealers create biases in specific sectors of the wheel. These sectors are easy to identify and ultimately exploit.

IDENTIFYING A POWER SECTOR

Most casinos nowadays feature electronic tote boards at each roulette table. These tote boards generally display the last 16 or 20 spin results in sequential order starting with the most recent number at the top of the display. Most use automatic laser detection devices to read the number from the wheel. A few rely on manual keypad inputs from the dealer. These tote boards serve a dual purpose for casino management. First, they provide an attractive signage to draw players into the game. Second, they provide electronic tracking to detect mechanical wheel biases. If a bias is detected, the wheel is generally taken out of service and repaired. To efficiently execute our Power Sector Method, you should try to play in casinos that feature tote boards. You can play without tote boards, but doing so would take more time.

Reading the Tote Board

Enter the casino prepared with a pencil, a small memo book (or roulette scorecard), and an illustration of a roulette wheel. Proceed to a roulette pit and study the most recent five or six numbers on each tote board. You do not yet know how many of the displayed numbers were thrown by the current dealer. So, it is prudent to assume that only the most recent numbers belong to him or her. It is important to keep in mind that you are playing into a specific dealer's bias, which will change from dealer to dealer. Hence, whenever a dealer change occurs, you must start anew.

As you study the last five or six numbers, look for a specific three- or five-pocket sector of the wheel that appears more than it should and follow along. Any five-pocket wheel sector represents 13 percent of a typical American double-zero roulette wheel with 38 pockets. Thus, if a game were to produce random results, then any defined five-pocket sector would hit 13 percent of the time, or 1 hit out of every 7.6 spins (on average). A three-pocket sector should randomly hit every 12.7 spins (on average). So, if you see a three- or five-pocket wheel sector hitting more than it should (1:12.7 or 1:7.6), then you have detected a bias.

A true Power Sector dealer will exhibit a very strong bias. A three- or five-pocket sector will hit with 1:3 or 1:4 frequency. Additionally (*this is very important*), a Power Sector dealer will often exhibit *two* Power Sectors, precisely 180° apart from one another. For example, if you observed a tote board with the following display (last 8 numbers):

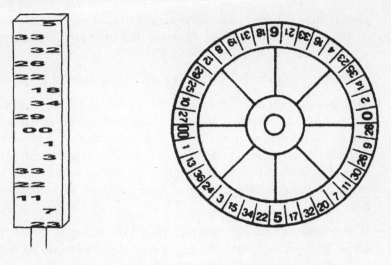

then you would have a very strong Power Sector dealer identified. Notice that the 5, 32, 22, and 34 are all within a five-pocket sector of the wheel. This five-pocket sector hit four times in eight spins (1:2), which is far greater than random probability and clearly indicative of a strong bias. Notice also that 33 and 18 are within a five-pocket sector *precisely 180° from the other Power Sector.* This sector hit twice in eight spins (1:4), which is also greater than random. This is a good example of a strong Power Sector dealer or game. They are not rare. You will find many games this strong and even stronger.

Here are some helpful additional tips to finding Power Sector dealers:

- You *can* play in casinos with no tote boards. Simply stand close to the wheel and record numbers as they hit.

- It is quite helpful to become familiar with the wheel. With a bit of practice, you will be able to spot sector biases with considerable ease. There is no need to memorize the wheel. Some players find it helpful to always orient their wheel illustrations in the same position when viewing it. For example, I always keep pocket 5 in the 6:00 position.

- The most common Power Sectors will occur around 0 and 00.

- Tote boards with laser sensors are 99 percent accurate and considered highly reliable. However, malfunctions do occur and you should occasionally verify the displayed numbers by looking directly at the wheel to ensure that the two match. Manual keypad type tote boards are highly *unreliable* and cannot be used. Fortunately, these manual types are not in widespread use.

- When determining the strength of a Power Sector dealer or game, there is no quantitative go/no-go measurement. As long as the hit rate is significantly above random, it is likely a true bias.

- A 180° secondary Power Sector is not always present with a primary Power Sector. But, when one is present, it provides added assurance.

Power Sector dealers or games can be readily found in most casinos at most times. However, during some sessions you may find the games are producing Power Sector opportunities; on other occasions, you may find that *no* games are playable. Power Sector games are clearly identifiable when they are there. Do not try to rationalize playing into a weak game just because conditions are bad. Simply wait for a better day.

BETTING TACTICS AND STRATEGY

Now that you know how to identify Power Sector opportunities, we will move on to the table play strategy. It's really quite simple. We flat-bet one unit on each of six inside numbers, *straight up*.

The first step is to identify the center of your Power Sector. From

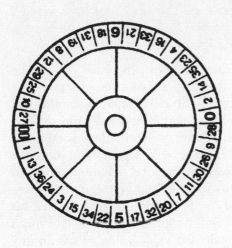

FIGURE 12: *Locating Your Play Numbers*

our previous example, the center is 5 (34-22-<u>5</u>-17-32). Identify the wheel number precisely 180° from your Power Sector center. From our example, the number 6 is 180° from 5.

These two wheel numbers (5 and 6) become the centers of the two three-pocket wheel sectors we will play each spin. In the Power Sector Method, we identify and play two three-pocket wheel sectors each spin. Each three-pocket sector is 180° apart from the other. Now identify the two wheel pocket numbers on either side of your two center numbers. From the example shown in Figure 12, we can see that 5 has 22 on one side and 17 on the other. The center number 6 has 21 on one side and 18 on the other. So, your six play numbers in this example will be 5, 6, 17, 18, 21 and 22.

Additional Power Sector Method Playing Tips

Now you know how to identify Power Sector dealers or games and how to play them. Here are a few additional tips for play:

- It is important to enter a game quickly once you have found a good one. The dealer may be due for a break, and you want to get as much playing time in against him or her as possible.

- The length of time that a game will remain strong will not be predictable. Sometimes a game will remain strong for an entire dealer shift. Sometimes a game will deteriorate as soon as you enter. You must be prepared to depart from a *bad* game quickly and ride a *good* game for all it's worth. Normally, a good game will produce a hit rate of 1:3, 1:4, or 1:5. A game that produces a hit rate of 1:6 or worse is not very good. Monitor your performance from the moment you enter and be prepared to leave at the first sign of deterioration. If you do not get your first hit within five spins, consider leaving right away. A 30- or 40-unit stop-loss should be your maximum in deciding to stay in any game.

- A bankroll of 250 units should suffice for all of your play. If you play in a good, disciplined manner, you will have playing sessions that produce several hundred units profit. Don't expect *all* sessions to produce at that high rate, but many will. It is suggested that you start with 50-cent or $1 units and double your unit size each time you win 250 units. Unit sizes of $5, $10, and $25 are achievable. Depart if you're drawn down 30 units from any high point.

- It is always a good idea to tip your dealer. The most effective way to toke with the Power Sector Method is by placing one unit on top of *your* bet "for the dealer." Place it on the center number of either of your play sectors. When the dealer hits, he or she makes 36 units (of course, you win too). Make sure the dealer knows the bet is being placed for him or her *before* the ball is released.

ADVICE FOR RECREATIONAL PLAYERS

Casino roulette is a great game that continues to grow in popularity, many of the larger casinos now offer 12 or more wheels. Many gamblers reading this book are looking to achieve an edge over the house—and the Power Sector Method will do it for you in roulette. But if you like to play just for fun, you probably don't want to take the time and effort to learn the Power Sector Method or anything else seemingly that complex. That's okay. If this is you, then we have several simple roulette playing techniques that will help to extend your playing dollars—and give you a fair shot at some significant winnings.

If you don't mind doing a little scouting and table-hopping, try the following:

- Play only in games that exhibit some identifiable trend. Look for obvious trends on the electronic tote board displays—repeating numbers. Then make your play choices based on the particular trend. For example, if you observe a tote board with two 23s, two 24s, and three 3s, then play in this game—and bet on 23, 24, and 3.

- Most trends occur for a reason. Many times they are *not* simple statistical fluctuations. And trends are more likely to *continue* rather than stop or reverse. Never bet against a trend!

- Limit your betting to a maximum of five units each spin. This will help maximize the life of your bankroll. If your session bankroll is $100, then risk no more than $5 per spin (five $1 betting units). This will give you 20 chances to latch on to a winning trend.

- If things don't go in your favor at a particular table, depart. Move to another trending table. Remember that if you're losing steadily in a game, that's a trend—and trends are likely to continue. Don't stay in a losing situation—it's more likely to stay bad than to turn good. Move to another table.

- When you find yourself in a solid winning situation, don't hesitate to increase the size of your bets. Move to two units where you were betting just one. If the game continues well, move up to three or four units each bet. Remember—*trends are likely to continue.*

If you don't want to scout or move around from table to table, simply sit in one game for the session and use these tips:

- Find a comfortable-looking table with at least a couple of other players. Enter the game and ask the dealer for a roulette scorecard. You'll need an illustration of the wheel for reference—and all scorecards include wheel illustrations.

- Play five individual numbers (inside numbers) each spin. The five numbers you play each spin will be the number that just won plus the two numbers on either side of the winning number, as they appear on the wheel. For example, if 2 was the number that just won, on the next spin you will bet 35, 14, 2, 0, and 28. This is 2 (the number that just won) plus 35, 14, 0, and 28 (the two numbers on either side of 2, as they appear on the wheel). You'll need the wheel illustration on the scorecard as a handy reference to determine your play numbers each spin.

- Most dealers will tend to repeat winning numbers—or come very close. This simple little playing method allows you to exploit what we call "the universal dealer repeat phenomenon." This method also allows you to play in a completely relaxed manner with a pretty good chance of winning.

- With this method, flat-bet five units each spin and you will likely be able to hold your own for an extended period of time. Expect to go back and forth with the dealer and to seldom find yourself down more than 100 units ($100 if you're playing $1 units—$5 total each spin). You'll need a bankroll of 250 units and you'll come out with profits after many sessions.

- If you find yourself down more than 100 units in any particular sitting, you must depart. The dealer actually has a tendency to *avoid* repeats. If you continue to play against this dealer, you'll simply lose more.

- If you happen to latch on to a dealer who has a *strong* repeat tendency, a dealer who hits your bets every three or four spins, then *go for the jugular*. In such a strong game you can really clean up. Each time you find yourself ahead 100 units, double your unit size. Instead of betting one unit per number, bet two units. Continue to raise your bets in this fashion as long as the dealer remains strong in your favor. In a game like this, you can win several hundred units and return home feeling on top of the world.

WHERE TO GO FROM HERE

Now you're armed with the basic understanding that casino roulette is a game of physics and mechanics—it is *not* a game of chance. And you know that the single most important factor in controlling the outcome of each spin is the dealer. You're also armed with the highly effective Power Sector Method. You are now better equipped to consistently beat roulette than 98 percent of all other players.

Spend a little time mastering the Power Sector concept. Learn it, then spend a session in the casino just observing and perhaps "paper playing" a few games. Don't actually play or risk money until you've had the opportunity to learn and practice a bit. But as soon as you feel ready, hit it!

Once you've seen it work and you've made some money, you may wish to consider contacting us for advanced information—perhaps even coming aboard as a Signature Series player. We're always researching the game and developing new, innovative playing techniques.

To bring yourself up to date with our roulette research, or to learn more about Signature Series Roulette, use the coupon in the back of the book to contact us for a *Signature Series Roulette* information newsletter.

Section Five

BACCARAT

Eighteen

BACCARAT

HISTORY

Historians have been unable to pinpoint the precise origin of the first card games, but they are believed to have been played over 2,000 years ago, before paper was invented. There has been evidence of card playing in ancient China, India, and Egypt.

As with dice, the Crusaders introduced cards to Europe in the fourteenth century, and although the church was soon preaching that they were the invention of the devil himself, Johann Gutenberg printed cards in A.D. 1440, the same year he printed his famous Bible. Consisting of 78 cards, the pack was called *Tarots*, and it formed the basis of today's deck of cards. The Tarots had four suits representing the four classes of feudal society. Swords, in Spanish *espadas*, from which we get spades, symbolized the nobility. Merchants were represented by coins, frequently square in shape, which, when turned on end, became today's diamonds. The sign for the serfs was literally a club, then called a baton, and today the cloverleaf-shaped sign is still called a club. The emblem for the church was the grail, or chalice, and from its characteristic shape developed our hearts.

Gutenberg's Tarot deck consisted of 22 *atouts*, or trumps — including a joker — and four suits of 14 cards each, with 10 numbered cards plus a king, a queen, a knight, and a valet or jester. Before the year 1500, the 22 atouts and the valet were dropped, although today in some games the five top-ranked cards are still called trumps, and in other games the joker (jester) is still used. Originally, the face cards were portrayals of actual personages, and slight traces of them remain to this day. The king of spades portrayed Charlemagne; the king of diamonds represented Julius Caesar; Alexander the Great was the prototype for the king of clubs. On the feminine side was Helen of Troy as the queen of hearts, Pallas Athena as the queen of spades, and the biblical Rachel as the queen of diamonds. Also honored from time to time were Joan of Arc and Elizabeth I, as well as a number of others. The knights, or jacks as they came to be called, were all patterned after famous soldiers, such as Sir Lancelot for clubs; Charlemagne's nephew Roland for diamonds; Hogier Le Danois, another Charlemagne lieutenant, for spades; and Etienne de Vignoles, who fought for Charles VII of France, for hearts. By 1492 the modern deck of cards as we know it had been established and was introduced to America by Christopher Columbus and his sailors.

Baccarat (pronounced *Ba-ka-ra* with short *a*'s and a silent *t*) was introduced in France during the reign of Charles VIII, around A.D. 1490. The game was devised in Italy by a gambler named Felix Falguiere, who based it on the old Etruscan rituals of the Nine Gods, who prayed standing on their toes to a blonde virgin who cast a *novem dare* (nine-sided die) at their feet. If her throw was eight or nine, she was crowned a priestess. If she threw a six or seven, she was disqualified from further religious office and her vestal status was summarily transmuted. And if her cast was five or under, she walked gracefully into the sea. Baccarat was designed with a similar partition (albeit with less dramatic payoffs).

Unfortunately, today it's the casino patrons who are usually destined to face a fate similar to that suffered by the would-be priestess when she cast a five or seven.

BACCARAT TODAY

The baccarat commonly played in the United States today is a combination of two variations of the game, European baccarat and chemin de fer (see the section titled "Baccarat Variations" on page 195 for a description of these two variations). The American version combines the best features of each. All players can bet on either the banker or player hand, and although the shoe rotates among the players, who take turns playing the banker hand, all wagers are covered by the casino, and the bank, subject only to a maximum-bet size, is relatively unlimited. This version of the game, originating in South America and played in England and other parts of the world under the name of *punto banco*, was introduced into the United States in the late 1950s by Tommy Renzoni after the Castro government closed all the casinos in Cuba.

Baccarat is a glamorous game aimed primarily at high rollers with an old-world air of graciousness. The game is played with special chips and higher stakes in a small, luxuriously appointed, roped-off area, and is dealt by tuxedoed croupiers in an atmosphere that is subdued and exclusive. Lady Luck is the predominant factor; whether you win or lose a bundle often depends on the turn of a single card, and the pay is dictated by chance, not by choice.

In most casinos, minimum bets are $20 or more (although a few casinos still open $5 games), although at certain times the minimum can be as high as $100. Maximum bets range from $1,000 to $2,000, but as usual, the larger casinos frequently raise the limit for well-heeled high rollers, and $500 chips are available for larger wagers. Because of the relatively high level of betting, baccarat is not a very popular game, and most casinos offer just a few tables.

If you are not concerned about the elevated level of betting, don't be frightened by the fast pace of the game—about two hands a minute. Baccarat is the easiest of all casino table games to learn, and no skill is required.

Actually, you don't need to know the rules to play, even if you are given the shoe to deal. The croupiers will show you where to bet, as well as when, where, and how to deal; they will also announce the winning hand. Everything is automatic.

As the cards are dealt, the banker, the croupiers, and the players do not have any choice about standing or drawing cards. The fixed rules of the game always dictate the play. There are no options, and no decisions to make other than the size of your wager and whether you choose to bet on the banker or the player hand. The game could not be any simpler.

Casino Crew

Standing at the center of the layout are two croupiers, each responsible for selling chips and collecting the losing wagers and paying off the winners on their respective half of the table. Printed on the table layout directly in front of them are 14 small boxes numbered to correspond with the player betting spots, and used to keep track of any commissions owed by the players.

Opposite these dealers sit another croupier, the *caller*, who directs the game. He tells the player with the shoe when to deal and to whom, and subsequently announces the winning hand. The caller also removes the first card in the shoe after the shuffle and turns it face up. The point value of this card, with face cards counting as 10 for this purpose, determines how many cards are to be *burned*, and the caller then places them in the discard slot in the table, just in front of him. Cards from completed hands are also collected by the caller and deposited in this slot. This continues until the cut card appears in front of the shoe, signaling a new shuffle after the completion of that hand.

Table Layout

The table is kidney-shaped to allow room for the dealers to reach out and handle both the bets and the cards. It is about 12 feet long and 3 to 4 feet wide (see Figure 13). The green baize covering is stenciled with a baccarat layout, providing numbered boxes in front of each chair for players to wager on either the banker or player

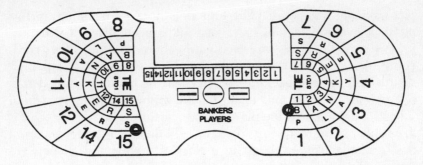

FIGURE 13: *Baccarat Table Layout*

hand. The places are numbered from 1 to 15, with 13 omitted, as few gamblers would be willing to sit and play at that traditionally unlucky spot.

Basic Play

The modern version of the ancient game of baccarat is played with 10 or more decks of cards. The decks are shuffled by the caller, cut by a player, and placed in a dealing box (the *shoe*), after the insertion of a cut card near the end of the combined decks to indicate the last hand. The shoe is then passed to a player at seat number one, who becomes the banker, although he may bet either hand. The shoe moves counterclockwise around the table each time the bank hand loses. Any player who becomes the banker may elect to pass the bank then, or at the completion of any hand, but to be eligible to deal, the banker must have at least a minimum bet on the table in either position.

After all wagers are placed, the banker alternately deals out four cards, face down, first to the caller, who slides the cards to a player (traditionally the largest bettor for that hand), and second to himself, sliding these banker's cards under a corner of the shoe. The player then turns over his two cards and tosses them to the caller, who announces the total. Following this, the banker uncovers the two cards that were tucked under the corner of the shoe, and the croupier calls out their value. The four suits have no meaning. At this point, a decision for the hand may have been reached with just these four cards. Tens and face cards count zero; all other cards count their point value; and if the hand totals more than 9, the left digit is disregarded; thus, unlike blackjack, no hand can bust. Totals of 8 or 9 are *naturals,* and are automatic winners, although a natural 9 beats a natural 8. If the player hand adds up to 6, 7, 8, or 9, or if the banker hand totals 7, 8, or 9, no additional cards are dealt and the hand that comes closest to a total of 9 wins and all bets are settled. Ties are a push; no money is exchanged and players are free to change their bets as they choose.

Frequently, the totals of the two hands require a third card to be dealt to the player, the banker, or both. Neither one has a choice in the matter because the rules are fixed. Optimal strategy has been developed for every possible combination of cards, and since as many as 15 players are wagering on just two hands, standing and drawing decisions are mandatory to avoid arguments over poor play. Remember, though, that neither player nor banker ever draws against a natural 8 or 9.

Rules for Player's Hand. If the rules require the player to stand on his initial two cards, the caller announces, "Player stands with (point total)." But if the player must draw, the croupier calls, "Card for the player." Only then does the banker deal a card face up to the croupier, who places it next to the first two cards as he announces the new total. The decisions for the player's hand are easy to learn. If the initial cards total 5 or less (including a zero, which would consist of two 10-value cards), draw one and only one card; otherwise stand. When the player hand is completed, the procedure for completing the banker hand is the same, but the rules for drawing or standing are a little more complicated.

Rules for Banker's Hand. Except for initial cards totaling 2 or less, which always require a draw, the decisions for the banker hand vary depending on the player's third card. Again, only one card may be drawn, and it's always taken if the banker's hand totals:

- 3 and the player stands or draws 1, 2, 3, 4, 5, 6, 7, 9, or 10.

- 4 and the player stands or draws 2, 3, 4, 5, 6, or 7.

- 5 and the player stands or draws 4, 5, 6, or 7.

- 6 and the player draws 6 or 7. The banker must stand if the player stands.

Notice that the rules can require the banker to draw even when his first two cards beat the player's final hand, and a third card can cause the banker's hand to lose. When both hands are concluded, the caller declares the winner, announcing the point total for each.

Because the inherent odds of the game favor the banker over the player, the casinos assess a 5 percent commission on all winning bets on the banker, so that the house advantage on either hand is about the same: 1.06 percent on the banker versus 1.23 percent on the player. The casino pays even money on all bets, which amounts to an overpayment on winning banker bets. But you don't have to worry about keeping track of the commissions on these bets. The dealers do this for you by placing tokens in your numbered commission box in front of them each time you bet and win on the banker's hand. The dealers collect the accumulated commissions while the cards are being shuffled for the next round, and they must be paid before you leave the table if you quit during a shoe. Always be aware of your commission indebtedness, and never bet your last chips before settling up.

BACCARAT VARIATIONS

European baccarat, baccarat en banque, and *chemin de fer* are all descendants of the original Italian game of *baccarat*, meaning "zero" and referring to the value of all 10-count cards. They soon became the exclusive games of the French nobility, not making their way to the public casinos for many years. The American version just described above is a combination of European and chemin de fer.

European Baccarat

In European baccarat, in addition to the player's standing or drawing on 5 as he pleases, the play of the dealer, who operates the permanent bank for the casino, is completely optional. In spite of these options, the decisions of the banker in almost all cases are exactly the same as required by the rules of play for American baccarat. Perfect employment of these options would not increase the fixed percentage in favor of the casino by 0.5 percent. In this game, players who choose to bet with the bank to win are charged 5 percent of their winnings on each bet.

Baccarat en Banque

The game of baccarat en banque is very similar, with the exception that one bank hand and two player hands are dealt. Frequently, the casino leases the bank as a concession to a syndicate that shares 50 percent of its monthly winnings with the casino, but in the event of a loss, the syndicate absorbs it all. In this version of the game, the player can bet on either or both of the player hands but never on the bank hand. The banker, a casino employee, can stand or draw as he chooses. Normally he will play according to the fixed American baccarat rules, but he can modify this procedure to enhance his chances of beating the player hand with the greatest amount of money bet on it.

Chemin de Fer

The basic difference in the game of *chemin de fer* (which is French for "railroad," and refers to the shoe moving around the table like a train) is that the bank rotates among the players. The house acts as a broker, collecting a fee from the winnings of each banker, and therefore assumes no risk. The player who is acting as banker cannot draw down any part of his original bank or subsequent winnings unless either the players do not subscribe to all the bank or, after the completion of any hand, the banker chooses to pass the bank. In this game, the player also has the choice of standing or drawing on 5, and the banker's play is completely optional. In any of these three games, the experienced American player who has observed the European game long enough to become familiar with the variations in procedure would be able to play a professional game just by using the American baccarat rules.

THE BACCARAT STREAK

A winning or losing session at baccarat is often defined in terms of "streaks." To illustrate this point, let's consider a case study involving a gambler I will call Mr. K. Mr. K. is a high roller. There is no doubt about it. I got to know him when he called me about participating in my Blackjack Clinic. He told me that he had dropped $25,000 playing baccarat and he wanted to find a way to win it back. I told him that I could teach him how to win at blackjack, but that I couldn't guarantee how much he'd win.

Mr. K. took the Blackjack Clinic and although he plays an excellent game of blackjack, Mr. K. is a gambler—he possesses the gambler's urgency to play for high stakes, so he can not resist the lure of the baccarat tables.

One day Mr. K. invited me down to observe his play at the baccarat tables. Agreeing to meet him in front of the baccarat pit prior to starting play, I arrived at the appointed time, only to find Mr. K. already in the game, looking very distressed. He had arrived two days earlier and was down about $10,000. Mr. K. expressed the usual gambler's lament about not quitting when he was ahead; at one point he had been up $5,000.

I sat down to play alongside Mr. K. Down to his last $500, he had used up his $4,000 credit line, so there was nothing he could do if he dropped that last $500. I watched it dwindle down to $50.

Now Mr. K. is a streak bettor, looking for a long series of wins in a row on either the bank or the players. He bets whatever has come up last until it loses. For example, if the bank wins, he keeps betting the bank until the players win. Then he jumps to the players until the bank wins, and so on.

Well, it was Mr. K.'s lucky day, because we caught a shoe with a lot of streaks, starting with 16 straight wins for the players. Mr. K's betting progressed from $40 to $500. As I was willing to risk only $100, my betting progressed from $20 to $200 in a conservative up-as-you-win progression as follows: 20-20-40-40-60-60-80-80-100-100-120-120-140-160-180-200.

This is one of the most amazing streaks I had ever seen in my 22 years of playing casino games. The odds of hitting 16 wins in a row are about 65,000 to 1. During the streak, Mr. K. prescribed certain things to keep it going: The player's cards were turned over by the same person each time; the banker's cards were always tapped against Mr. K.'s chips; the only conversation allowed was in conjunction with the bet size; and counting chips was prohibited. But this streak was not the last good thing to come out of this fantastic shoe: Three or four other streaks of five or six wins occurred, and at the end of the shoe, Mr. K. had recouped his $10,000 and had won another $1,000 to boot. I had multiplied my $100 by about 17.

There is a moral to this story, and that is that the people who sell baccarat systems use streaks like this to prove that baccarat works, to appeal to the greed of unsuspecting gamblers in their sales literature. The aftermath of the story is that Mr. K gave all his winnings back and then some at the baccarat tables in the weeks after this session. He became a disillusioned gambler and has not visited a casino in years. I strongly agreed with his decision; in fact, I encouraged him to give up gambling.

THE HOUSE ADVANTAGE

These kinds of streaks are what the baccarat players pray for, but unfortunately there is no way to predict them. To my knowledge, there is no way to get a statistically verified advantage in this game. Sure, the game is streaky and you can get lucky and ride one as I did in the story about Mr. K., but there is no way to predict these streaks whether they are on the player's side, on the banker's side, or chop back and forth.

But, interestingly, the strategies employed by most baccarat players are to detect the streaks or trends in the shoe and bet that they will either continue or reverse. Capitalizing on the short-term streaks or trends that may occur, a high roller could win in excess of $5 million in a single session. But more often he will lose that and more. A loss of $20,000,000 has been reported for one session.

Here is a review of the house edge that eventually catches up to even the most astute of baccarat players:

- Banker hand—1.06 percent

- Player hand—1.23 percent

- Tie—14.05 percent

A BETTING STRATEGY FOR BACCARAT

If you want to have some fun and play like these whales and try to catch a streak like Mr. K's, here is the procedure:

1. Establish a bankroll of 20 to 50 units—preferably $5 each. Recognizing that baccarat is usually a high-limit game, you may have to risk 20 units of $25 each or $500.

2. Get a scorecard when you enter the game, and chart each decision using the standard notation of P for player and B for bank.

3. Bet single units, or $25 a hand, for the first 20 to 30 hands of the shoe.

4. Watch carefully how the game unfolds during these first 20 to 30 hands, looking for obvious trends in the game. For example, is the shoe "choppy," with P and B alternating back and forth for many hands in succession; that is, P, B, P, B, P, B? Is the

game exhibiting short-term streaks like P, P, P, B, P, B, B, B? Or perhaps you detect another choppy trend like B, B, P, P, B, B, P, P, B, P.

5. Baccarat players, including high rollers, look for trends like these and then bet them either to continue or reverse. For example, if the first 30 hands are choppy, a gambler might start betting for streaks to occur; that is, he continues betting whatever the last hand was. If it was P, he bets P; if B, he bets B. He might start raising his bet on this next hand, anticipating a favorable streak. On the other hand, if a gambler notices a streaky shoe in these first 30 hands or so, he might bet for these streaks to reverse. You have to decide which way to go when you notice a trend. Do you go with it or against it? Remember, we're gambling here and there is no way of predicting for certain what will happen.

6. If you're in a streaky shoe, with both P and B participating on short-term streaks, play these streaks to continue with a *paroli of three*. This simply means parley your bet twice, going for a win of three hands in succession. You bet $25 and win. Let it ride and bet the $50. If it wins, let it ride once more and bet the $100. On any loss or after winning the three hands in a row, revert to a one-unit bet. To start your paroli of three, you could either bet whichever won on the last hand (if P wins, start with P), or go the other way (if P wins, start with B). Just be consistent.

7. If you're in a choppy shoe, bet that whichever side won the last hand will not win three more hands in succession. If P won, bet $25 on B. If you lose as P wins again, bet $50 on B; if P wins again, go for it and bet $100 on B. I If you win any of these three hands, you've won $25. If you lose all three, you've lost $175. Time to withdraw from the game and sit out a few hands or wait for a new shoe.

8. Some players believe that if P is dominant in the first 30 hands, winning maybe 20 or more hands, that things will even out

with B dominating the next 30 hands of the shoe. (Note that 30 hands represent about half a shoe.) If you wish to use this idea, I recommend the conservative approach of flat-betting the last half of the shoe on whichever side is due to come back and even out.

Section Six

CASINO POKER, OTHER CASINO GAMES, AND GAMBLING ON THE INTERNET

Nineteen

CASINO VARIATIONS OF TRADITIONAL POKER

HISTORY

Poker is the quintessential American card game, just about as American as apple pie. It was even played by our founding fathers, and another form was played by Native Americans before the arrival of the Europeans.

In the nineteenth century, every state and territory west of the Mississippi River had casinos. And most, if not all, offered poker. Poker was played on the gambling riverboats cruising the Mississippi in Mark Twain's day (just as it is today).

In the late nineteenth century, poker was played in plush casinos in New York and other big eastern cities. When the New York City casinos were shut down, the casinos moved upstate to Saratoga Springs, where poker was played in "Lake Houses," because many of the casinos were located near a lake.

At the turn of the century, the famous gambler Richard Canfield owned the most popular casino in Saratoga Springs, called The Casino. Many of the richest industrial giants of the time played in high-stakes poker games at this location.

Around 1910, political reform and a progressive movement swept many corrupt local governments out of office and closed down all casinos, so, like alcohol soon after, poker was relegated to the back rooms and "speakeasies" of the day, where it flourished.

Gambling was declared illegal in Nevada in 1912, and it wasn't until 20 years later that the state realized it was their only real source of income, and legalized it once again. But the casino operators soon realized they could make far more money with slots, roulette, blackjack, and craps, so poker was soon bumped to the back room areas of the casino.

Bugsy Siegel, who is given credit for defining the Las Vegas Strip, did not have poker in mind when he built the Flamingo in the late 1940s. With few exceptions, the Strip hotels built through the 1960s and 1970s did not even offer poker. You had to go to the "sawdust joints" and smoky back rooms of the downtown casinos to find a game. And in those days, the locals mainly played poker.

But things changed when Benny Binion, owner of the Horseshoe Casino in downtown Las Vegas, designed a tournament called "The World Series of Poker." This tournament, with its $10,000 buy-in and winner-take-all format, drew many of the professionals from the private poker circuits around the country and began popularizing the game. With the media publicizing the tournament, the tourists and Friday night poker players watched in amazement as huge sums of cash changed hands.

Hollywood picked up this national interest in poker and made a number of poker-themed movies that were quite popular and boosted interest in the game. Suddenly, poker was "in" in Las Vegas and the rush was on by the big Strip hotels to build fancy poker rooms to attract the high rollers in search of a game.

In the late 1980s and through the 1990s legalized gambling exploded across America. The main reasons were the passage of the Indian Casino Gaming Act by Congress in 1987 and the approval of statewide casino gaming in Mississippi. And this led to the great gambling boom experienced all through the 1990s, which will probably continue well into the new millennium.

This proliferation of casinos led to increased competition for the gambling dollar—attracting many new gamblers who either weren't interested or didn't want to take the time to learn traditional games such as blackjack, craps, and roulette. The casinos wanted to exploit this new market by offering fun games that were easy to play. Realizing that most gamblers knew at least the basics of poker, but would probably be too timid to sit in on a traditional poker game, they designed and introduced the poker variation games described in this chapter.

These variations were an immediate success. With their built-in bonuses, they attracted the less experienced players who love the excitement of getting back three, four, five or more times their basic bet. Corporate casino management and stockholders loved these poker variation games too, because they possess a higher house edge and therefore yield a much higher profit than the other table games.

CASINO POKER VARIATIONS

The four most popular of the poker variation games will be discussed in this chapter: Caribbean Stud, Let It Ride, Three Card Poker, and Pai Gow Poker. With the exception of Pai Gow Poker, it is impossible to gain a player advantage in these games. And in Pai Gow Poker, only the most skilled professional with a huge bankroll is able to achieve this advantage. But the games are fun and easy to play and represent an interesting diversion for recreational and serious gamblers alike.

These games differ from traditional poker in that you are not playing against the other players—in Caribbean Stud, Three Card Poker, and Pai Gow Poker you are playing against the dealer; in Let It Ride, you are simply trying to get the best hand possible, no dealer involved. All you need to know about traditional poker to understand these games is the hierarchy of poker hands, which is shown in Table 3. All games are played on a blackjack-like table, which will accommodate up to seven players, and all are played with a 52-card deck (in Pai Gow Poker, a joker is added to the standard 52-card deck). To keep the game moving along, an automatic shuffling machine is used. Cards are dealt face down and you are not allowed to show your cards to the other players.

Royal flush: A, K, Q, J, 10 of same suit

Straight flush: straight of same suit

Four-of-a-kind: four like cards (4-4-4-4)

Full house: three of a kind and a pair

Flush: all cards same suit

Straight: 5 cards in sequence (6-7-8-9-10)

Three-of-a-kind: (three like cards)

Two pair: (7-7; J-J)

Pair: (Q-Q)

High card: Ace is high, then K-Q-J-10-9-8-7-6-5-4-3-2

TABLE 3: *Hierarchy of Poker Hands*

If two players have a full house, the hand with the higher three-of-a-kind wins. If two or more hands have flushes, the flush with the higher-ranked card wins. Ditto straights. If two hands have three-of-a-kind, the hand with the higher three-of-a-kind wins. For two pairs, the hand with the higher pair wins.

Caribbean Stud

In this game, you are playing against the dealer and against a house edge of a little over 5 percent on the ante bet and about half that on the hand bet which, as explained in a moment, is double that of the ante bet.

Step 1. You place a bet in the ante square and, optionally, you can make a side bet of $1 in the jackpot slot. Each game has a jackpot meter that shows the value of the progressive jackpot. This is a side bet and has nothing to do with the play of the hand against the dealer. The hands necessary to win the progressive jackpot are shown in Table 4. This table is representative of most casinos. If more than one player hits the royal flush, each shares equally in the progressive payout.

Royal flush: 100 percent of progressive payout

Straight flush: 10 percent of progressive payout

Four-of-a-kind: $500

Full house: $100

Flush: $50

Usually no payout for hands lower than flush.

TABLE 4: *Progressive Jackpot Bonus Payouts for Caribbean Stud*

Step 2. The dealer deals five cards face down, to each player and himself, except his last card is dealt face up.

Step 3. The players check their cards and make one of two decisions: (1) They stay in the game if they think they can beat the dealer; (2) they surrender their hand and lose the ante bet if they do not believe they can beat the dealer. If they surrender, that is the end of their action for this round of play.

Step 4. The remaining players place a bet that is double their ante in the bet square. Then they place their cards face down on the table.

Step 5. The dealer turns over his facedown cards and arranges the five cards in the best possible poker hand. For the game to proceed from this point, the dealer must have a hand that is ace-king or better. If not, the game is finished; the dealer pays off all the antes without looking at the players' hands. The bets are *pushed*, meaning neither the player nor the house wins. The players take back their bets. If the dealer doesn't qualify in this step, and terminates this game, players who have a hand that qualifies for a piece or all of the progressive jackpot must announce this fact to the dealer. Otherwise, your facedown cards are scooped up, and you lose your bonus money. An example of a game terminating hand is J, 10, 7, 3, 2. If the hand were A, K, 9, 4, 3 or better (see Table 3) the game proceeds.

Step 6. With a hand of ace-king or better (the dealer qualifies), the dealer compares his hand against each player's hand. If his hand is better, he collects both the ante and the bet. If the player's hand is better, the dealer pays the ante at even money and pays the player's hand according to the typical payout shown in Table 5. If the dealer doesn't qualify with an ace-king or better, he pays off the ante and pushes the bet.

One pair or less: 1 to 1

Two pair: 2 to 1

Three-of-a-kind: 3 to 1

Straight: 4 to 1

Flush: 5 to 1

Full house: 7 to 1

Four-of-a-kind: 20 to 1

Straight flush: 50 to 1

Royal flush: 100 to 1

TABLE 5: *Typical Payouts for Caribbean Stud (Paid If Dealer Qualifies)*

That's it. The game is that simple to play. Your only three decisions are (1) whether to bet on the progressive jackpot; (2) how much to bet on this hand; and (3) whether to stay in the game or surrender your hand.

The odds against winning the jackpot are astronomical, almost like winning a lottery, so I advise against playing this game. But, if you are playing just for fun, are ahead for the session, and want to throw away a dollar on every hand, then go for it.

Caution. If you win the progressive jackpot or portion thereof, you must show your hand if the dealer doesn't qualify. If you don't, he'll scoop up your facedown cards and you've lost out!

Bet Size. Regarding your bet size, use my advice in Chapter 2 about the betting decision. Realize that you're playing against a house edge of 5 percent and go easy. My advice for playing your hand is simply fold if your hand is less than an ace-king. If it is ace-king or better, play the hand. There are complicated strategies for playing your hand depending on the dealer's up-card. But they take very little off that big house edge of 5 percent. So forget about them and enjoy the game!

Let It Ride

In this game, you are playing for the best poker hand possible (the dealer is not involved), and the house edge is a little less than 3 percent. Your five-card poker hand consists of three cards dealt to you and two "common" cards that all the players use to make up their five-card hands. When you play the game, notice the three betting squares on the layout labeled "1," "2," and "$" because they figure prominently in the rules of play described here.

Step 1. To start, the players place three bets, one in each of the three betting squares. You will learn shortly that you will have the option of removing two of these three bets depending on the strength of your hand and the risk you wish to take.

Step 2. The dealer deals three cards face down to each of the players and two "common" cards, also face down. The players look at their three cards without showing them to the other players.

Step 3. The players now decide to take back their number "1" bet or "let it ride." To let a bet ride, the player tucks his three cards under his wager or lays the hand down behind the number "1" bet.

If the player wishes to take the bet back, he scratches the felt as signal to the dealer to return the bet. Do not reach for it yourself.

Step 4. After all the players have decided on their number "1" bets, the dealer turns over the first of the two common cards. With this additional information, the players now decide whether to take back their number "2" bets or let that bet ride in the same way as the number "1" bet. At this point in the game, it is possible that you may only have one bet at risk, the "$" bet, but that bet may not be taken back. Or, if you've let one or both "1" and "2" bets ride, you have one or two bets at risk going into the next step.

Step 5. The dealer turns over the second common card and the players' five-card hands are now complete—their three cards and the two common cards. Your hand is paid off according to the typical payoff schedule shown in Table 6. Note that if your hand is less than a pair of 10s, you lose. Also note that if you let one or both of your "1" and "2" bets ride, you could be collecting on or losing one, two, or three bets.

Royal flush: 1,000 to 1

Straight flush: 200 to 1

Four-of-a-kind: 50 to 1

Full house: 11 to 1

Flush: 8 to 1

Straight: 5 to 1

Three-of-a-kind: 3 to 1

Two pair: 2 to 1

Pair of 10s or better: 1 to 1

TABLE 6: *Typical Payouts for Let It Ride*

Bet Size. Aside from your bet size for the "1," "2," and "$" bet boxes, the two decisions you make in this game are whether to let the "1" and "2" bets ride. On the "1" bet, I recommend letting it ride only if your three cards contain a pair of tens or better (higher pair or three-of-a-kind) or if your three cards are of the same suit (the possibility of a flush) or are in sequence; for example, 6, 7, 8 (the possibility of a straight). Otherwise, take the "1" bet back. On your "2" bet, clearly you will let it ride if you opted to let the "1" bet ride with a pair of tens or better. With a three-card flush or three-card straight, let your "2" bet ride if that first common card improves your hand to a pair of 10s or better or to a four-card flush or four-card straight. Otherwise fold your hand and take back the "2" bet.

Three Card Poker

This game is growing in popularity because it combines the best of Caribbean Stud and Let It Ride. Your objective is to beat the dealer's hand but, in this case, you have a three-card hand instead of a five-card hand. You also have the option of a side bet called Pair Plus, which is paid out independent of your decision against the dealer, with a fixed bonus schedule, similar to a slot machine. There are three types of bets, including Pair Plus—the other two are Ante and Play. The rules of play are described here. Note that in this game, a three-card hand of three-of-a-kind beats a straight or flush because three like cards are more difficult to get than a three-card flush or straight. The house edge is a little less than 2.5 percent.

Step 1. The players make their Pair Plus and Ante bets. Either one or both bets may be made.

Step 2. The dealer deals three cards to each player and himself. After you look at your three cards, you must decide whether you wish to "play" the hand or fold and take no further part in this hand. If you fold, you lose your ante bet.

Step 3. To stay in the hand, you make a bet in the Play box equal to your ante bet. Now you are in the game and playing against the dealer.

Step 4. After all the players have made their decisions, the dealer turns over his three cards and determines whether he has a qualifying hand. If the dealer does not have at least a queen-high or better hand, the players win the ante bets and have their play bets returned. If the dealer qualifies with queen-high or better, he settles all the hands.

In a dealer-qualifying hand, if your hand is better than the dealer's, you collect even money on the ante and play bets. If not, you lose both bets. Note that even if you lose both the ante and play bets with an inferior hand, you do collect a bonus on the ante bet even with a losing hand. A typical bonus payout schedule is shown in Table 7.

Straight flush: 5 to 1

Three-of-a-kind: 4 to 1

Straight: 1 to 1

Flush or lower: zero

TABLE 7: *Typical Ante Bonus Payouts for Three Card Poker*

If you have made a Pair Plus bet, you are paid according to the schedule in Table 8. If your hand doesn't qualify for a bonus, you lose the Pair Plus bet. Note that it has nothing to do with whether you win or lose your ante and play bets. Also note the three-card hierarchy: Three-of-a-kind is more difficult to get than straights and flushes, and a straight is more difficult to get than a flush.

Straight flush: 40 to 1

Three-of-a-kind: 30 to 1

Straight: 6 to 1

Flush: 4 to 1

Pair: 1 to 1

All other hands: player loses

TABLE 8: *Typical Pair Plus Bonus Payouts for Three Card Poker*

Your decisions in Three Card Poker are whether to make the Pair Plus bet, how much to bet on Ante, and depending on your three cards, whether to fold or make the Play bet.

Since there is no possibility of achieving an advantage in this game, I recommend avoiding the Pair Plus bet until you are comfortably ahead from the Ante and Play bets. Then, with luck on your side, make a Pair Plus bet when you feel lucky or have a hunch on that next hand.

As far as the Play bet is concerned, it seems logical that you follow the dealer. If the dealer must have a queen-high or better to qualify, you should, too. Therefore, fold your hand if it's less than a queen-high. Let the dealer have the Ante bet and avoid the risk of losing that play bet on an inferior hand.

Pai Gow Poker

Pai Gow Poker is a cross between the ancient game of Chinese dominoes and poker. It is played with a 53-card deck—the standard 52 cards plus a joker that can be used as an ace or to complete a straight or flush—on a blackjack-size table. Seven cards are dealt face down to each player. The players pick up their cards and "set" their seven cards into a five-card hand and a two-card hand.

Hand Ranking. The ranking of hands in Pai Gow Poker differs from standard poker in two ways: (1) Because of the joker, the high hand is five aces, which beats the royal flush. (2) In some casinos, A-2-3-4-5 ranks as the second-highest straight behind A-K-Q-J-10 and ahead of K-Q-J-10-9. Be sure to check this rule before you begin play. In the two-card hands, there are no flushes or straights, only a pair or high card. The highest two-card hand is A-A; the lowest is 2-3.

Rules of Play. Before play begins, it must be determined which player is to receive the first card. The traditional way of doing this is for the banker to shake three dice in a cup three times and then place the covered shaker on the layout. (Some casinos use a random-number generator with digital readout to determine which spot gets the first hand.) The dealer removes the shaker cover to reveal the numbers. Then, starting with the bank, the dealer counts each seat counterclockwise, including the dealer's spot, and continues counting until the number equal to the sum of all three dice is reached. That player or dealer receives the first seven-card hand. Seven-card hands are then dealt, counterclockwise, to each of the seven playing positions regardless of whether a player occupies that position. Thus, 49 cards are dealt out of the 53-card deck for each game.

Setting Hands. After the hands are dealt and the unused cards at the open spots are picked up by the dealer and placed in the discard tray, the players set their hands. When setting the two hands, *it is very important for the player to set the five-card hand with a higher ranking than the two-card hand.* If the two-card hand has a higher ranking, the hand is declared "dead" and you lose your money. An example of a hand declared dead is K-Q-9-6-2 as the five-card hand and 3-3 as the two-card hand. A pair, of course, is a better hand than king-high.

After a player finishes setting the two hands, they are then placed facedown in the designated spots on the layout.

For the players to win, their five-card hand and their two-card hand must beat the dealer's five-card hand and two-card hand. The dealer wins if his five-card hand and two-card hand beats the player's five-card hand and two-card hand. If the hand splits—that is, one hand wins and the other loses—no money changes hands. If one of the dealer's hands is the same as the corresponding player's hand, and the dealer wins the second hand, the dealer wins and collects the bet. If one of the dealer's hands is the same as the corresponding player's hand, and the player wins the second hand, the hand is declared "no decision" and no money is exchanged.

Part of the house edge, about 1.3 percent, comes on these tie or "copy" hands that the house wins. The house edge is enhanced to about 3 percent by a 5 percent commission or "rake" collected by the dealer on each winning bet.

There is one more aspect of Pai Gow Poker that makes it different from every other casino game—the players have the option of banking the game. I don't advise this unless you have a very large bankroll or are coming off a big winning session and feeling lucky.

Before discussing the banking decision, let's address the more important decision of setting your seven cards into a five-card hand and a two-card hand. As you analyze your seven cards, you must keep in mind that both the five-card and two-card hand must win for you to win the bet. Therefore, you want to set the strongest possible hands you can, which might mean breaking up a good five-card hand to strengthen your two-card hand. And in setting the two hands, the player must always keep in mind that the five-card hand must be a higher-ranked hand than the two-card hand. Otherwise the hand is disqualified and the bet is automatically lost, regardless of whether the player's two hands beat the dealer's two hands.

Let's take an example to show how the hand-setting decision works. Suppose you hold the following cards: A-A-A-10-8-3-2. Would you set the three aces in your five-card hand, or break them up as a pair of aces in your five-card hand and an ace high in your two-card hand? Do you see the problem? If you keep the three aces and the 3-2 as your five-card hand, then there is the good possibility that your two-card hand of 10-8 will be a loser. If you break the aces up, you have a better chance of winning both hands.

There are strategies for how to set most seven-card hands, but even the simple ones require memorization and time to learn. If you're interested in mastering this game and reducing the house edge to a minimum, I suggest getting a copy of the *Gambler's Book Club Catalog* and looking under the Pai Gow Poker category.

Basic Strategy. In the meantime, here is a simple strategy to get you started on the seven-card Pai Gow Poker hands indicated:

- *High card*: Set the second- and third-highest cards as your two-card hand, keeping the remaining five cards for your five-card hand.

- *Pair*: In a hand with no straight or flush, set the pair in the five-card hand and the two highest of the remaining cards as your two-card hand.

- *Two pair*: Set the low pair in the two-card hand and the high pair in the five-card hand.

- *Three pair*: Set the high pair in the two-card hand and the two lowest-ranked pairs in the five-card hand.

- *Three-of-a-kind*: Set three queens or lower in your five-card hand. For aces and kings, set two of them in your five-card hand and the other one in your two-card hand.

- *Straights, straight flushes, and flushes*: Set them in your five-card hand and the remaining two cards as your two-card hand.

- *Full house:* Set the three-of-a-kind in your five-card hand and the pair in your two-card hand.

- *Four-of-a-kind*: Set one pair in each hand, unless your four-of-a-kind is 2s through 6s—in which case you set them in the five-card hand, with the two highest-ranked of the remaining three cards as the two-card hand.

If you're uncertain about how to set your hand, ask the dealer for help. Dealers have a prescribed strategy for setting their own hands which they will be happy to share with you and help you arrange your seven cards into the five-card hand and two-card hand with the best chance of winning.

Banking Decision. Now to the banking decision. Banking the game means that the player is prepared to cover all the other players' bets for the next round of play. If more than one player wishes to act as banker, the bank rotates from player to player. Acting as banker doesn't mean that you're actually dealing the cards (the dealer still deals), just that you're prepared to cover all the bets on the next round. If the players do collectively bet more money than you have in front of you, you pay them off in turn, paying counterclockwise, until your money runs out; the remaining hands are then declared as no-play hands and the bets are returned to the players. Most casinos will not let any one player bank every hand; the usual policy is every other hand if no other players wish to bank. Ask your dealer for the policy of the casino if you're interested in banking the game.

Some gambling writers say that it is possible to achieve a small advantage over the casino in Pai Gow Poker. This advantage is so small as to be negligible, but to complete your understanding of Pai Gow Poker, I'll describe how this edge might be achieved.

Disregarding the rake, the banker has an advantage over the players of a little over 1 percent. So the first step to achieving a small theoretical advantage is to act as banker as often as you can to garner this 1 percent edge. If no other players wish to act as banker, the casino will usually let you bank every other hand (but, again, verify their policy with your dealer). Another factor that affects your advantage is bet size. When you're the banker, you want the other players to bet high because you have the advantage. But, when you're the player and betting into the house or into the other players acting as banker, bet small because now you're playing with a disadvantage.

The advantage you achieve as banker is not actually real because, as banker, you still have to pay the commission or rake on each winning bet you collect from the other players. The best that you can hope for, depending on the ratio of your small bet when player to your hoped-for larger bet sizes of players betting against you as banker, is to break even. In other words, as banker, the money you win on tie or "copy" bets is just about offset by the rake you pay on each winning bet you collect. Your advantage, then, must come from your superiority over the other players of setting your seven cards into a five-card hand and a two-card hand. If you're banking against less skillful players, you're looking at a possible edge of under

0.5 percent, probably less than that or maybe zero if the other players use optimal strategies for setting their hands.

Not enough to really get excited about, but there you have it. I recommend playing the game as a diversion and to have a little fun. Your serious play should be dedicated to blackjack, craps, and roulette, where a much higher advantage—a real advantage—can be attained.

Twenty

CASINO VARIATIONS OF BLACKJACK

The casinos have been offering variations to the traditional black-jack game since the early 1980s. Their objectives are threefold: (1) to make it impossible to gain an advantage by card counting; (2) to make the game more appealing than traditional blackjack to the recreational player, the average gambler; and (3) to increase the casino's edge and thus increase the house profits.

Some of these games catch on, while others don't and are quietly put to their death. To give you a broad understanding of these blackjack variation games, I describe four of them in this chapter — each with different reasons for being introduced, and each with its own unique characteristics.

SINGLE-DECK BLACKJACK DEALT TO THE BOTTOM

One of the most interesting variations was a single-deck game offered by Bob Stupak at the old Vegas World Casino (since demolished and replaced by The Stratosphere). He realized that card counters were always looking for an edge in this game by getting deeper penetration into the deck. They wanted more cards to be dealt before shuffling, and wanted as high a betting spread as possible (the ratio between the high bet, when the counter had the advantage, and the low bet, when the dealer had the advantage), so he gave them all they wanted and then some. First, his dealers dealt 51 of the 52 cards. Second, he let the counter bet as little as $5 and as high as $2,000 — a 400 to 1 betting spread. Counters flocked to this game when it first opened, but the knowledgeable ones quickly found out that it was a sucker's game — blackjack, instead of paying 3 to 2, paid only even money, even if the dealer had one, too. This one rule change was more than enough to offset the deck penetration and the steep betting spread. Still, many card counters couldn't resist this game, believing they could still beat it, even with the even-money blackjack, but to no avail; the game was extremely profitable to the old Vegas World. This game is now history. But interesting, don't you think? If they ever resurrect this game, don't let history repeat itself for you!

DOUBLE EXPOSURE BLACKJACK

Another game that was extremely popular in the 1980s and is still around in a few casinos is called Double Exposure. In this variation, the dealer shows both his cards, instead of one card up and one card down. In a traditional game, this rule of knowing the dealer's exact hand would give even the basic strategy player a huge edge. For example, think about a stiff hand, such as a 16, against a 10 up-card. Basic strategy says you should hit. But in Double Exposure, seeing that the dealer's hand is also stiff, you stand and leave the dealer with the higher chance of breaking because he must hit 16 or less. The catch in this game is when both hands are the same — a push in traditional blackjack, with no money changing hands. In Double Exposure, the dealer wins all pushes, a huge house edge of about 9 percent. Picture yourself with a 19 against the dealer's 19; what do you do? If you stand, you lose the tie bet. You must hit the 19 with the extremely small chance of catching the ace or deuce. Even though this game is very appealing to the recreational player, there is no way you can realistically beat it. I recommend that you avoid it.

MULTIPLE ACTION BLACKJACK

This is one of my favorite variations of blackjack. In this game, you are playing your dealt hand, with two or three bets, against three different dealer hands, but all starting with the same up-card. The game begins with the players placing either two or three bets in three betting circles in front of each player's seat. Let's say the dealer deals himself a 5 while you're sitting with a 15. Basic strategy says you should stand. After all of the players make their decisions, the dealer completes this hand. Let's say he breaks. This is Hand 1, and the dealer pays off the players left in the game (those who have not broken and lost). Now comes Hand 2. You play your same hand, but the dealer must deal himself a new hand starting with that same 5 up-card. This hand is completed and then a third hand is dealt in the same way, with you keeping your same hand and the dealer dealing another hand to that 5 up-card. Going back to your hand of 15, if you hit that 15, let's say against a 10 up-card, you lose all three bets and now must wait for the round of three hands to be completed and another to begin.

This game is really fun when you find yourself in a dealer-breaking table (see Chapter 6 for a discussion). The characteristics of a dealer-breaking table are low up-cards that turn into stiff hands (12–16) and then the dealer breaks. Instead of winning just one hand, now you're winning three. The winnings can pile up fast in a multiple-action game. If you play this game, use basic strategy to play your hands, and use the betting tactics described in Chapter 3.

SPANISH 21

This blackjack variation game is becoming extremely popular and should be around for a while. Spanish 21 offers the player-favorable rule of doubling down on any number of cards, not just your first two. So, if you draw 3, 4, 2, a hand totaling 9, you can double down. Another player-favorable rule is surrender. Surrender your first two cards and lose only half your bet.

But how would you like to play in a blackjack game with bonuses paid for the following hands:

- A five-card hand equal to 21 pays 3 to 2

- A six-card hand equal to 21 pays 2 to 1

- A seven (or more)-card hand equal to 21 plays 3 to 1

- A three-card hand of 6, 7, 8 of mixed suits pays 3 to 2

- A three-card hand of 6, 7, 8 of the same suit pays 2 to 1

- A three-card hand of 6, 7, 8 of all spades pays 3 to 1

- A 7, 7, 7 hand of mixed suits pays 3 to 2

- A 7, 7, 7 hand of the same suit pays 2 to 1

- A 7, 7, 7 hand of all spades pays 3 to 1

Very attractive, aren't they? But, as usual, there is a catch (naturally) — a multi-deck Spanish 21 game contains no 10s! Every 10 has been removed (just the 10s, not the jacks, queens, or kings) from the six- or eight-deck game. If you're playing perfect multi-deck basic strategy, with no advantage play strategies, I estimate the casino advantage against you at about 3 percent. Frank Scoblete, in his book *Armada Strategies for Spanish 21*, says he can reduce the house edge to a little less than 1 percent if you learn his hand-playing strategy, which capitalizes on the favorable rules.

Is the game worth it? I don't think so. I believe your time is better spent with the advantage strategies in this book even if you're an occasional gambler. But if you like to make lots of decisions and if you like the bonus-hand payoffs in Spanish 21, you might want to give it a try as a fun diversion from the traditional game.

Here are some of the decisions confronting the Spanish 21 player:

- Should I double down on a three-card hand or a four-card hand?

- Should I take a hit with my four-card 15 against a dealer 6 up-card in hopes of catching a 6 for a 21 and collecting the 3-to-2 bonus?

- Should I go for that third 7 and the bonus even if the dealer shows a 5 and has a higher chance of breaking on this hand?

- Should I surrender my two-card 15 against the dealer's jack up-card?

Basic Strategy

If you do decide to take a shot at this game, here are a few things to keep in mind:

1. Use the basic betting tactics described in Chapter 3.

2. The most favorable rule in this game is the one allowing the player to double down on any number of cards instead of just the first two. When your first two cards are soft, such as with an ace or if your first two cards total less than 8, always anticipate a possible three- or four-card double-down hand.

3. Because the six-deck shoe has 24 fewer high cards with the 10s removed, your double-down basic strategy rules should be adjusted to eliminate a few double-down hands. This is because of the smaller chance of the player catching a high card to complete the double-down hand, and because of the smaller chance of the dealer catching a high card to break a stiff hand. Therefore, if your two-card or multi-card hand totals 9, double-down on dealer up-cards of 5 and 6 only, not 3–6. For a hand totaling 10, double-down on 4–7 only, not 2–9. And, for a hand totaling 11, double-down on 3–8 only, not 2–10.

4. For soft hands—hands containing an ace, which can be counted as either 1 or 11—you have a choice of going for the

bonus on the five-, six-, seven (or more)-card 21 or looking for the opportunity of doubling down. Which do you choose? Opt for the double-down. The reason is that to catch the bonus, your hand must total 21 exactly. It happens sometimes, but not often enough to pass up a good double-down bet. Use basic strategy for doubling down on soft hands. Some soft hands will naturally lead to the opportunity of the multi-card 21 bonus. For example, if you are faced with a 10 up-card with an A, 2, and hit this hand with an ace for a soft 14, then a 2 for a soft 16, you're in position for a "free shot" at the five-, six-, or seven (or more)-card 21. Suppose you catch a 2 for a soft 18? Basic strategy says hit against the 10 so you have another free shot at the 21. But now, hitting this 8 or 18 with a 7, for example, what do you do? Now you're sitting with a five-card 15. Basic strategy says hit this hand against the 10 so you still have one or two more shots to catch the multi-card 21 as part of your basic strategy play.

5. As I described in the previous paragraph, let the bonuses come as part of your traditional basic-strategy play. In other words, do not hit a breaking hand in hopes of catching a multi-card 21, a 7, 7, 7 hand, or a 6, 7, 8 hand. For example, if you are dealt two 7s and the dealer's up-card is a 6, follow the basic strategy of splitting instead of going for the bonus hand. Another example: If your hand is 3, 2, 3, 8 against a dealer up-card of 6, you might be tempted to go for the five-card 21 bonus, but I don't recommend it. Play basic strategy and stand. The same advice holds for a hand of 6, 7 against a 5; don't be tempted to go for the 6, 7, 8 bonus. Follow basic strategy and stand.

6. Basic-strategy rules for hitting the stiff hands of 13–16 should be adjusted to factor in the fewer 10s in the game. Play these stiff hands the same way you would play a 12—hit on a dealer up-card of 2 and 3; stand on a dealer up-card of 4, 5, and 6.

7. Add one hand to the basic-strategy surrender rules described

in this chapter—surrender a pair of 8s against a dealer up-card of ace.

8. If you're in the game and in doubt about the basic-strategy adjustments recommended here, play basic strategy.

There you have it—four examples of variations to traditional casino blackjack games. As time goes on, I suspect the casinos will continue to introduce new variations to traditional blackjack. If you play them, take care! One thing you can always be sure of is that they will be very advantageous to the house.

$\mathcal{T}$*wenty-one*

GAMBLING ON THE INTERNET

The Internet is a global information and communication network. Gamblers can talk to other gamblers anywhere on the planet and access gambling-related information from a variety of sources. Just as with the explosion of gambling-related books, sources of gambling information are exploding on the Internet. Newsgroups on gambling provide a forum for gamblers on just about every casino game, especially blackjack. A plethora of Web sites offering advice and gambling systems are out there in cyberspace, visited by thousands of gamblers. Some of this information is free; some you pay for.

GAMBLING NEWSGROUPS AND WEB SITES

Do gambling-related newsgroups really dispense information? Information is facts and data. But too many Internet providers of gambling information are providing their own opinions, opinions not based on facts or data. Is this solid information? Sometimes. But, depending on the provider, in many cases it's *misinformation* and can lead the gambler down the wrong path—a path that could lead to wasted time and lost money.

As you might expect, much of the information exchanged in gambling newsgroups pertains to gambling systems. "What do you think of so-and-so system?" is an example of an inquiry often posted. The person who posted is thinking about buying or acquiring the system and wants validation from other gamblers that it does, in fact, work.

If you post a comment like this and ask for responses, how do you assess value, or lack thereof, in the opinions you receive? You don't know the source; many Internet users don't use their real names. Or they may have their own ax to grind to try to persuade you to see things their way. Many times you will get conflicting opinions. Or the system seller himself may respond to your comment and you would have no way of knowing.

The responses you get may be any of the following:

- An opinion based on hearsay, of what others on this newsgroup think

- An opinion based on reading the sales material or reading about the system in a book

- An opinion based on purchasing or acquiring the system and reading the system materials

- An opinion based on one or two sessions of trying the system out in the casino

- An opinion supported by sufficient casino sessions to generate results data that are statistically significant

- An opinion based on computer simulation

These opinions may be wrong or they may be right. Many will be in a gray area with lack of factual, supporting evidence.

How, then, do you evaluate this kind of "information" or "data" received from your posting on one or more newsgroups? Do criteria exist that can be used for evaluation? Yes, they do, but describing them here is beyond the scope of this book.

What you can do, however, is always insist on the source of the information, and proof to back it up.

I would recommend against purchasing any system advertised on the Internet, but if you are considering a purchase, ask to see proof that it works beforehand. And ask for references of system users — not their E-mail names and addresses, but their real names and voice phone numbers.

This explosion of gambling "information" is a problem and presents a hurdle for both the serious and recreational gambler to surmount. After all, that's one reason why you're reading this book.

INTERNET CASINOS

As this book is being written, casino gambling is proliferating on the Internet. Dozens of casinos are offering gaming for fun as well as real action at their Web sites. Internet casinos are all located offshore, many in the Caribbean.

From your computer, you can bet on sporting events and horse racing; you can play blackjack, craps, roulette, and other table games; and you can play slots and video poker. All you need is access to the World Wide Web. Entering the word *casino* on any of the major search engines will yield hundreds of responses. Or, before you enter the Net, read some of the reviews in the gaming magazines to get an idea of which casinos you may wish to visit.

But wait! What's the catch? Is it really this easy? Sitting comfortably in front of your computer, at home or at the office, at any time of the day or night, and bellying up to a blackjack game offered by a casino located in the Dominican Republic, for example?

My simple but strong advice can be expressed in two words: Be careful!

Be very careful of the casino you release your credit card to. Are they a viable company and licensed by the government of the country in which they operate? Is their bankroll big enough to sustain severe losses? Are they currently under investigation by the United States, a state government, or any foreign government?

Be careful about the casino evaluations you read in the various gaming magazines. Many magazines evaluate and rate Internet casinos. But thumb through the pages of this same magazine and you'll find an ad for the rated casino. So how objective do you think the rating will be?

Be careful about the games you play. Are you getting the correct odds? Are the games legitimate? How do you know, for example, that in a six-deck blackjack game more dealer-favorable 5s have not been added to the game? Or that player-favorable 10s, jacks, queens, or kings have not been removed?

Many casinos claim to be audited by big, nationally known accounting firms — the same firms that oversee many state lotteries. They also claim that these audits are online and ongoing, not one-time annual events. Okay, I can buy this. But, having spent a former career in the computer industry, I know that it is possible for a skilled programmer to bypass or short-circuit the auditing software.

Skimming Scams?

What I am getting at here is the possibility of online skimming. Picture this scenario in an offshore casino: One 5 randomly added to a six-deck shoe game as the online audit software is bypassed for just a few hands at random. A 5 increases the dealer's chance of winning because it will turn any dealer stiff hand — 12, 13, 14, 15, and 16 — into a standing hand. Sure, it's a very small added edge, but over thousands of hands, it adds up big dollars skimmed by the casino from this game.

Here's another one: In an online craps game, the table gets hot and players load up on placing the numbers; there's a lot of money on the table working for the players as the shooter throws the winning numbers and avoids the losing 7. The casino's smart software detects this situation, executes a nanosecond bypass of the audit software, and rolls the losing 7.

If you're in this game, how would you know that you had been cheated? How would the audit software know? By monitoring the "hold" or profit on this game and detecting a larger-than-expected casino win? But where's the money that the casino won on that illegally thrown 7? In the old days, the hoods would walk right into the counting rooms in the Vegas casinos and pick up a satchel of

$100 bills. Now, we're looking at much more sophisticated skimming methods using state-of-the-art software to direct the skimmed money to the casino's private bank account in this foreign country, or maybe to a bank in Nevis or the Canary Islands with confidentiality policies stricter than Switzerland's.

I could give you examples for any casino game, but I think you get the idea.

Don't get me wrong—I'm not saying all Internet casinos are crooked. There are legitimate operators in cyberspace. Just make sure you're dealing with one of them before you place your first bet.

Also, before you make that first bet, you need to check out any laws that may prohibit online gambling in your state, or any federal laws that make online gambling illegal. Several are pending as this book goes to press.

Let me give you a reason *not* to make that first bet, a logical reason not to gamble on an Internet casino, a reason that is inherent in the themes of this book—the games are generated by computer. This means that random-number generators are used to create the spin of the wheel, the toss of the dice, or the cards that are dealt at blackjack or baccarat.

So if these games are truly random, or close to it, they would not be as predictable as a blackjack game with a biased shuffle, a roulette wheel at which you can read the dealer's signature, or a craps table where you can execute a controlled throw. In a real casino, you can secure an advantage. That's what this book is all about. Is this possible in an Internet casino? Not now. In the future? Maybe. I have researchers working on this challenge as I write these words. To get a status report on this cutting-edge research, request a free Update Report with the coupon in the back of this book.

INTERNET SPORTS BOOKS

Let's now turn our attention from the Internet casinos to the Internet sports books. They are proliferating just as fast as, if not faster than, the Internet casinos—there are over 100 in operation as of

1999. The sports books are catering to the multibillion-dollar sports betting industry in this country, and the only place you can get a bet down legally is in Nevada. Before the Internet, illegal bookies could be found in most cities who would take your bet. Many have been driven out of business by the flourishing offshore sports books, which may be legal in the country in which they operate, but not in the United States because making a wager via telephone across state lines is prohibited by federal law. The key word here is *state*. When you call an offshore sports book via an 800 number, you're obviously crossing state lines, but your call is made across international lines and ends up in a foreign country. Right now the feds have no way of cracking down on these offshore books except to shut down their 800 numbers, which is difficult to do without backup legislation. But laws are being introduced in the U.S. Congress as this book goes to press. Their aim is to shut them down, because bringing unrestricted gambling into the home could cause some extreme social problems, especially if teenagers gain access to the sports books. Sports book operators are considered expatriates; if they return to this country, they could be arrested for taking those telephone calls across state lines and breaking federal law. They're hoping for regulation instead of termination. We'll have to wait and see what happens.

Other than the online skimming, most of the caveats above apply here as well. But there is one difference between Internet casinos and Internet sports books that you should be aware of, and that is the time factor. In an online casino, a gambler can make hundreds of bets at a blackjack game, for example, and slowly get ground out of a $500 bankroll as the house edge continues to work. But this same $500, bet on sporting events, could be just one bet or perhaps 5 or 10 bets. Suppose the sports bettor is operating with a $550 bankroll and makes 10 bets on 10 football games, each $55 to win $50. It's pretty hard to lose all 10 of these bets; more than likely the bettor will go five and five, winning $250 on the wins and losing $275 on the losses. So it's taken the sports book three hours to win $25 from this bettor while, in the same duration, the casino gambler could have made hundreds of bets and been ground out of his entire $500.

The point I'm making pertains to the sports book's bankroll. The sports book operator is much more likely to suffer losing days than the casino operator. It's possible that sports bettors loading up on one game could make a serious dent in the book's bankroll. Sure, the book could lay this off to a larger operation, but many don't and end up gambling themselves. If they lose, they may have trouble paying off if you ask for money from your account. This is why it's even more important to check out your sports book than an online casino. I am aware of many cases in which the sports book reneged on paying off sports bettors — especially big bettors betting hundreds or even thousands of dollars per game. Here is just one example: A gambler could not retrieve $9,000 from his sports betting account in an offshore sports book. Why? It turned out that the casino was spending thousands of dollars on legal fees to fight a state government agency attempting to close them down in that state. They were cash-poor and were waiting for fresh funds from unsuspecting sports bettors to bail them out. Be careful! I suggest getting a bank reference if you decide to open an offshore account.

The future direction of gambling on the Internet is anyone's guess. We'll have a much better idea when current state and national legal issues are resolved, including the outcome of the Federal Gaming Commission, which was created by Congress to study the effects of gambling on the American economy and lifestyle. All of this will be covered in the Update Report mentioned previously.

In the meantime, be careful or, better yet, avoid the Internet casinos and sports books altogether.

Appendix

COURSES AND SERVICES OFFERED BY JERRY PATTERSON

ABOUT THE AUTHOR

Jerry Patterson has been playing casino blackjack since 1956. He entered the gaming field full-time in 1978 when the Atlantic City casinos opened. He played professional blackjack for several years in the 1980s and managed several blackjack teams during that period. He is the author of five gambling books. Founded in 1978, his gaming company, Jerry Patterson Enterprises, Inc. (JPE), a.k.a. Jerry Patterson's Blackjack Clinic, is the oldest and most successful company in the gambling instruction and services field.

Through this company and via his former syndicated casino gaming column published in newspapers and magazines internationally, Patterson has taught millions of gamblers the rudiments and the fine points of how to win at blackjack, craps, and roulette. He has been involved in researching and developing winning gambling systems since the early 1960s. An example of a notable accomplishment in the blackjack arena is the first shuffle tracking method. The initial version was published in 1985 in his book *Break the Dealer*.

A final version was published in 1990 in his book *Blackjack: A Winner's Handbook*.

His attention turned to casino roulette and then to casino craps in the 1990s. Much of that work is documented in this book.

THE JERRY PATTERSON CLIENT NETWORK

In 1998, JPE celebrated its 21st year in the gaming instructional business, longer than any other gaming school. There are some very important reasons for this longevity, but the main one is hands-on follow-up support. Patterson and his instructors have always been accessible to their students and clients — by phone, fax, seminars, and E-mail, and in the casino. For example, the TARGET 21 Blackjack Course features free Question and Answer Seminars three or four times a year in Las Vegas and Atlantic City, free of charge to previous clients. Patterson's instructors also check out their students' play in the casino — in supervised four-to-five-person groups.

This follow-up support wouldn't work, of course, if the methods were not winning methods. JPE has sponsored an ongoing research program since the early 1980s in blackjack; since the early 1990s in roulette; and, beginning seriously in the mid-1990s, in controlled throws and rhythm rolls in craps. We keep our systems current and always stay a few jumps ahead of the casinos.

Another reason for Patterson's success is an unconditional refund policy beginning with the first course you buy and extending to any course or service you buy from JPE.

On page 239 there is a brief description of home study courses and services. Contact JPE for complete details on purchasing them direct, using the coupon at the back of this book.

BLACKJACK COURSES

Blackjack: A Winner's Handbook

This book has been in print since 1978, has been through three editions, has sold over a quarter of a million copies, and is now the second best-selling blackjack book of all time (behind Ed Thorp's *Beat the Dealer*). It contains a complete course on basic strategy and card counting.

PARTIAL CONTENTS

- A four-phased non-count strategy, which minimizes losses while enabling you to score in those games where the dealer is breaking and the players are winning.

- Strategies and tactics for card counters including three never-before-published strategies for beating the dealer in today's changing game conditions.

- A complete handbook of learning drills for basic strategy, card counting including basic running count, and conversion of the running count to the true count for betting and hand play decisions.

- Seven chapters on the evolution of blackjack systems in the 1980s, including Team Blackjack, shuffle tracking, concealed computers, hole card play, biases, and reasons why card counting doesn't always work and what you can do to avoid losing.

- Tips for becoming a pro or semi-pro player, including a seven-step winning program.

The TARGET 21 Home Study Course

TARGET 21, which stands for Table, Research, Grading & Evaluation Technique, is a method for finding winning tables. We call these tables player-biased tables or dealer-breaking tables. They result from biases caused by the non-random shuffle.

The TARGET 21 Method takes up from where this book leaves off in teaching you how to find a winning table. This method is not marketed to the gaming public. Patterson would rather have you, an educated reader and player, make the initial contact for more information. Based on the information you receive, if you feel you can extend your knowledge and increase your winnings, Patterson and his instructors will be happy to work with you.

PARTIAL CONTENTS

- How to select a winning table — the 12-step scouting process
- How one TARGET 21 superfactor maximizes the chances of winning at this table
- When to leave the table with profits in hand
- How and why TARGET 21 solves the problems associated with card counting
- How to use TARGET 21 to pick tables where the count really works
- Why the "wash" makes certain games off-limits
- Understanding the different types of shuffles and how they work to your advantage or disadvantage
- Special drills for TARGET 21 in-casino practice
- Questions and answers from a live TARGET 21 classroom session
- How to increase your profits by using a disciplined documentation method
- Money management and betting alternatives for varying levels of risk

- Tips for finding the "home-run tables" where the dealer breaks hand after hand. Ninety minutes in the casino with one of Patterson's instructors and a small group of other students

The Blackjack Masters Home Study Course

TARGET 21 is the blackjack players' winning foundation. Blackjack players desiring advanced instruction should consider acquiring this home study course.

PARTIAL CONTENTS

- How to anticipate player-favorable rounds and bet up into them; a higher percentage of big bets won yields a higher table win rate, more winning sessions, and more dollars per hour of play.

- How to anticipate dealer-favorable rounds and reduce the bet to table minimum to keep your losses low and not eat into the profits you've already accumulated in this game.

- How to read the dealer's hole card by using clump card techniques—not every time, but often enough to give you a tremendous feeling of power. Visualize yourself at third base, predicting a low hole card under the 10 up, standing on a stiff hand and watching the dealer break.

- How to predict whether the next card out of the shoe will be high or low. How many times have you doubled down on an 11 only to see the dreaded low card come out of the shoe? Now you'll have a much better chance of doubling into a high card because you'll be predicting them!

- How to predict whether the next shoe will be favorable. How many times have you left a table and wondered about that next shoe? Now you'll have the ability, based on game reading, to stay in a profitable shoe, or leave and avoid that losing shoe.

- How to beat the ShuffleMaster machines in the shoe games. This technique is so effective that blackjack masters scout for these machines now as opposed to avoiding them.

- How to build a $10,000 bankroll by flat-betting green chips. This is only one of the many innovative betting tactics you will learn.

- How to document each blackjack table you play and use the information to analyze your play, detect problems, and take corrective action.

The Blackjack Masters Course is a mentoring program, including seminars, networking, and one-on-one consultation in deciding on your own personalized learning program. Learning materials are 15 hours of audiotape instruction and a detailed training manual.

CRAPS INSTRUCTION

The Craps Home Study Course

The advantage method and home study course are called Sharp-shooter Craps. The course consists of videotape and audiotape instruction combined with a 70-page instruction manual and supervised dealer school and in-casino practice sessions. The instruction is aimed at four linchpins.

First Linchpin: The Set. I've shown you how to set the dice in this book, but there is one optimal set that reduces to a minimum the chances of rolling a losing 7. With this patented set, one die would have to rotate at a faster or slower speed than the other for the 7 to occur.

Second Linchpin: The Rhythm Roll. I've also described herein how to develop your rhythm roll. The home study course will save you some time in developing this skill. In it, you'll learn what we call the "perfect pitch" because of its accuracy and its penchant for avoiding the losing 7. Of course, it's not really perfect, but we strive for perfection and settle for excellence.

In these first two linchpins, you learn the set, the grip, and the throw in less time than if you tried on your own.

Third Linchpin: The Zone. In learning how to roll, you're developing what we call muscle memory. This takes some practice. When you've developed this muscle memory skill, you want to be able recall it at will—when you're in the casino and ready to roll for the money. This is like a batter stepping up to the plate to make contact with the ball or a basketball player getting "in the groove" and sinking shot after shot. We've developed a simple mental technique to put you in the groove or "in the zone," as we call it, every time you throw.

Fourth Linchpin: Betting and Money Management. Just because you have an advantage doesn't mean you're going to win. You have to know how to bet to exploit it. The betting techniques I've incorporated in this book were taken right out of the home study course manual. But there are many more all designed to suit the playing styles and aversion to risk of all classes of gamblers. For example, in the home study course you will learn low-risk betting tactics designed to retrieve your "start-up money" and let house money finance your play as you go for the long hand. For the more aggressive players, we show you how to "go to green" in just three or four rolls and then exploit the hot hand.

The Sharpshooter Craps course also involves you in our client network. This networking includes periodic supervised practice sessions in dealer schools at which Patterson's trained instructors, including Sharpshooter, critique your throw and make sure you're doing everything "by the book." They don't stop there—each instructional session concludes with supervised play in the casinos.

ROULETTE INSTRUCTION

The Signature Series Home Study Course

The Signature Series course teaches you how to detect and qualify the dealer signature in many games with the use of a quick, simple "charting" procedure. Players exploit the signature with an advantage over the casinos by placing bets on five inside numbers, "straight up." Players exploit their advantage by using either a conservative flat-betting approach, which can yield substantial units per hour of profit, depending on skill level and casino conditions; for example, the number of spins per hour is dependent on the number of players in the game, or on one of several aggressive up-as-you-win approaches which can multiply the hourly profit derived by flat-betting!

One of the most attractive features of the Signature Series methods are that no large bankrolls are required. Players can begin with a bankroll of no more than $250. In casino locations that offer low-stakes games, a starting bankroll of only $60 or $70 is adequate.

Signature Series methods are unique — like nothing you have seen before. They have nothing to do with mechanically biased wheels, biased sectors, or extended up-as-you-lose betting schemes. The methods are completely legal and involve no cheating or use of hidden electronic equipment. They are quick and simple and can be effectively employed even in the fastest of game conditions.

The instructional program is an easy-to-follow home study format. It consists of an easy-to-understand manual, two audiotape supplements, and a series of "practice pack" exercises, complete with a regulation-size table layout felt and a supply of casino-quality chips for home practice. In-casino signature identification and validation are part of the program.

HOW TO CONTACT JERRY PATTERSON:

By phone: (800) 257-7130
By phone: (775) 265-9224

By mail: Send this form to:
Jerry Patterson Enterprises, Inc.
P.O. Box 236
Gardnerville, NV 89410-0236

Or fax this form to: (775) 265-0085

E-mail: *jpe21@aol.com*

Dear Jerry,

[ ] Send me a copy of your book *Blackjack: A Winner's Handbook* to the address below. Enclosed is $12 plus $3 for priority mail shipping, a total of $15.

I want more information about becoming an Advantage Player; please send detailed information on your systems, methods, and home study courses I have checked below, which pick up from where this book leaves off:

[ ] Blackjack/TARGET 21 Home Study Course
[ ] Blackjack Masters Home Study Course
[ ] Sharpshooter Craps Home Study Course
[ ] Signature Series Home Study Course for casino roulette

Also send me the free information I have checked below:

[ ] Update Report on Internet Casinos and gambling-oriented Web sites
[ ] Wallet-sized blackjack Basic Strategy Card for: [ ] shoe game
     [ ] single-deck game
[ ] Information about the Casino Gamblers' Clinics, which you and your instructors periodically offer in locations near casino cities.
[ ] Break-even calculation for 6 and 8 place bets

Name: _____

Street Address: _____

City/State/Zip: _____

Telephone Number with Area Code (optional): _____

Credit Card # ($15.00 for book): _____ Exp. Date: _____

Signature: _____